# Folens

## Book 4

# LANGUAGE WORKS

# Contents

# The Real Thing

And there was the river. It swirled past, cold and unfriendly in the early light. The hand set Lucy down among the weeds of the bank, and she watched amazed as the gigantic figure *waded* out into midstream, till the water bulged and bubbled past those thighs that were like pillars of a bridge. There, in the middle of the river, the giant woman kneeled, bowed and plunged under the surface. For a moment, a great mound of foaming water heaved up. Then the head and shoulders hoisted clear, *glistening* back, and plunged under again, like the launching of a ship. Waves slopped over the bank and soaked Lucy to the knees. For a few minutes, it was like a giant sea beast out there, rearing up and plunging back under, in a boiling whirlpool of muddy water.

Then abruptly the huge woman levered herself upright and came ashore. All the mud had been washed from her body. She shone like black glass. Her great face seemed to *writhe*. As if in pain. She spat out water and a groan came rumbling from her.

"It's washed you," cried Lucy. "You're clean!"

But the face went on trying to spit out water, even though it had no more water to spit.

"It burns!" Lucy heard. "It burns!" And the enormous jointed fingers, bunched into fists, rubbed and squeezed at her eyes.

Lucy could now see her clearly in full daylight. She gazed at the giant tubes of the limbs, the millions of *rivets*, the funny *concertinas* at the joints. It was hard to believe what she was seeing.

"Are you a robot?" she cried.

Perhaps, she thought, somebody far off is controlling this creature, from a panel of dials. Perhaps she's a sort of human-shaped submarine. Perhaps ...

But the rumbling voice came up out of the ground, through Lucy's legs:

"I am not a robot," it said. "I am the real thing."

And now the face was looking at her. The huge eyes, huge black pupils, seemed to enclose Lucy – like the gentle grasp of a warm hand. The whole body was like a robot, but the face was somehow different. It was like some colossal metal statue's face, made of parts that slid over each other as they moved. Now the lips opened again, and Lucy almost closed her eyes, she almost shivered, in the peculiar vibration of the voice:

"I am Iron Woman."

*Ted Hughes*

 **Look up the words in italics in the dictionary section at the back.**

Write down their meaning.

 **Answer these questions.**

**1.** How did Lucy get to the river?

**2.** Why did the gigantic figure plunge into the water?

**3.** Why did Lucy get wet?

**4.** Can you think of the reason why water would have such an effect on this strange creature?

**5.** Why do you think Lucy did not run away?

**6.** Describe the strange woman's face. How was it different from the rest of her body?

**7.** If the Iron Woman is not a robot what do you think she is? Why do you think she says, "I am the real thing."?

 **Similes.**

There are five examples in this story where the writer gives us a picture of the Iron Woman by comparing it with something else. When writers use 'like' or 'as' in this way, it is called a simile. Write down which aspect of the Iron Woman the following refer to:

**1.** ... like black glass

**2.** ... like the launching of a ship

**3.** ... like pillars of a bridge

**4.** ... like a giant sea beast

**5.** ... like the gentle grasp of a warm hand

Think of two more similes of your own to describe the Iron Woman.

 **Choose which words below describe the passage and write them down.**

| gentle | exciting | slow | well-written | descriptive |
|---|---|---|---|---|
| frightening | mysterious | humorous | adventurous | difficult |

Add some words of your own.

Now write a paragraph saying what you like or dislike about the passage.

# Sentences

 A sentence is a group of words which makes complete sense on its own. It begins with a capital letter and ends with a full stop.

 **Answer the following.**

**1.** Read again the first paragraph of 'The Real Thing'. How many sentences are there?

**2.** Look at the third sentence of the first paragraph. It is quite long. Try to rewrite it as three sentences (you will need to make one or two minor changes).

**3.** The author has used sentences of various lengths and has taken care to ensure that they fit in well with each other. In one case he has used a sentence which, strictly speaking, is not a 'sentence' – it does not make sense on its own. Can you spot it?

**B** **Write six sentences to describe this picture.**

**C** **Rewrite this paragraph, showing correct sentencing, capital letters and full stops.**

the Inuits are clever hunters they travel over the snow and ice on sledges drawn by a team of fierce dogs called huskies these dogs have a sharp sense of smell and can find the breathing holes of seals in the thin ice the Inuit kills the seal with a harpoon as soon as it appears in summer the Inuit hunts for walrus in a frail kayak the kayak is a light wooden boat covered with sealskin

# Capital Letters

● As well as being used to begin sentences, capital letters are used:

1. To begin the names of weekdays, months and festivals. e.g. We celebrated Christmas Day on a Monday last December.

2. To write the word 'I'. e.g. Anne and I are best friends.

3. To begin the names of people, titles of people and the titles of books, plays, films, etc. e.g. Sarah Brown and Professor Davis shook hands with President Clinton. Steven Spielberg directed 'Jurassic Park'.

4. To begin the names of places and words made from the names of places. e.g. The Spaniard visited Paris, the capital of France.

5. To begin direct speech. e.g. Paul said, "Meet me at the shops at seven."

 **Rewrite the sentences, inserting capital letters.**

1. the expert said to mary, "i will try to answer all your questions."
2. peter and frank speak fluent portuguese.
3. though i supported italy, i had to admit that the brazilians deserved to win the match.
4. by the time doctor kennedy arrived, poor aunt lucy was in severe pain.
5. i went to see 'aladdin' at a cinema in berlin.
6. the swedish tourists visited disneyland on new year's day.
7. the amazon is the world's largest river but egypt's nile is the longest.
8. roald dahl wrote the book 'charlie and the chocolate factory'.
9. my uncle tom is coming home from new york on thursday.
10. I'm interested in books about dracula.
11. my indian penfriend, indira, is coming on friday.
12. captain avis is flying to switzerland in march.
13. i asked you a question, "did you see the match on friday?"

 **Here is an excerpt from the diary of Captain Wonder. Rewrite it, inserting capital letters and full stops.**

saturday, may 1st, 2088: i received a phone call last night from president connors in the white house he said "good luck, rita, everybody here in the united states is right behind you" mr connors also spoke words of encouragement to the other two members of the crew, bill winters and fatima iqbal i looked out of the window all morning as we orbited mars red-coloured gas was rising everywhere and i felt very nervous about the prospect of the landing on monday i'm not surprised the ancient romans chose mars as their god of war if there are any martians living down there i hope they're a friendly people

# Using Your Imagination

● Our mind is a storehouse of ideas which we can tap into at any time.

For example, let's take the word 'castle' as a starting point. Ponder over it a while and write each word that comes to mind. We end up with a lot of new words ... and a lot of new ideas!

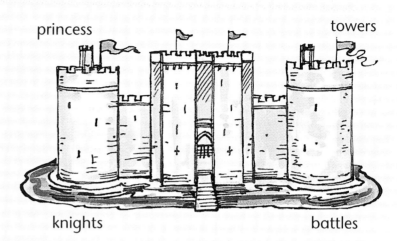

princess     towers

knights     battles

 **Write the words that come to mind as you look at these pictures.**

(1)

(2)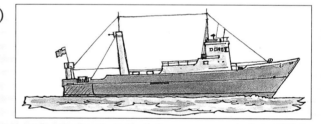

 **Creative guessing.**

You are woken in the middle of the night by a knocking at your front door. You open it to find your best friend standing there in a dressing gown. Write three good explanations for his/her strange behaviour.

 **Write what you think the Earthlings and the Martians said to each other. What happened next?**

# The Marrog

My desk's at the back of the class
And nobody nobody knows
I'm a Marrog from Mars
With a body of brass
And seventeen fingers and toes.
Wouldn't they shriek if they knew
I've three eyes at the back of my head
And my hair is bright purple
My nose is deep blue
And my teeth are half yellow half red?
My five arms are silver with knives on
them sharper than spears.
I could go back right now if I liked –
And return in a million light years.
I could gobble them all for
I'm seven foot tall
And I'm breathing green flame from my
ears.
Wouldn't they yell if they knew
If they guessed that a Marrog was here?
Ha-ha they haven't a clue –
Or wouldn't they tremble with fear!
Look, look, a Marrog
They'd all scream – and SMACK.
The blackboard would fall and the
ceiling would crack
And the teacher would faint I suppose.
But I grin to myself sitting right at the back
And nobody nobody knows.

*R.C. Scriven*

 **Answer these questions.**

**1.** Why are the children not able to see the Marrog?
**2.** Describe the Marrog and draw a picture of the creature.
**3.** Say whether or not you like the poem and why.

 **Make up a creature that only you know about that lives in your classroom.**

Describe what it looks like. Give it a human personality. (This is called personification.) Now write a story or a poem about it.

# Wagon Train

That day began like any other.

At four o'clock in the morning, when the rising sun stood like a red-glowing ball above the grey landscape, the guards fired off their rifles, as a sign that the hours of sleep were past. Women, men and children streamed out of every tent and wagon; the gently smouldering fires from the previous night were *replenished* with wood, and bluish-grey clouds from dozens of *plumes* of smoke began to float through the morning air. Bacon was fried, coffee was made by those who still had some. The families which could still cook maize mush for the children thought themselves lucky.

All this took place within the 'corral', that was to say inside the ring which had been made by driving the wagons into a circle and fastening them firmly to each other by means of the shafts and chains. This formed a strong barricade through which even the most vicious ox could not break, and in the event of an attack by the Sioux Indians it would be a *bulwark* that was not to be despised.

Outside the corral the cattle and horses cropped the sparse grass in a wide circle. At five o'clock sixty men mounted their horses and rode out of the camp. They fanned out through the crowds of cattle until they reached the outskirts of the herd; once there, they encircled the herd and began to drive all the cattle before them. The trained animals knew what those cracking whips meant, and what was required of them, and moved slowly in the direction of the camp. There the drivers picked their teams of oxen out of the dense mass and led them into the corral, where the yoke was put upon them.

From six o'clock until seven, the camp was extra busy; breakfast was eaten, tents were struck, wagons were loaded, and the teams of *draught* oxen and mules were made ready to be harnessed to their respective wagons and carts. Everyone knew that whoever was not ready when the signal to start was blown at seven o'clock would be doomed for that day to travel in the dusty rear of the caravan.

Seven o'clock. Every driver was at his post. A bugle rang out! The guide and his escort mounted their horses; the four wagons of the leading section rumbled out of the camp and formed the first column, the rest took their places with the regularity of clockwork, and the caravan moved slowly forward over the broad *plateau*, far above the foaming river. A new hard day had begun.

*Rutgers van der Loeff*

10

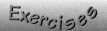

 **A** **Look up the words in italics in the dictionary section at the back.**

Write down their meaning.

 **B** **Answer these questions.**

**1.** What is a corral?

**2.** Why did the men select the oxen from the herd?

**3.** Who ate 'maize mush'?

**4.** What happened to those who were slow to start?

**5.** List some examples to show that this was a well organised group of travellers.

**6.** Explain why you think these people have set out on the wagon train.

**7.** Which do you think is the most descriptive sentence in the story? Say why.

 **C** **Summarise in single sentences what happened in the camp at each of the following times:**

a) four o'clock   b) five o'clock   c)  six o'clock   d) seven o'clock

Use no more than sixty words altogether.

 **D** **Change the narrator:**

We call the storyteller or 'voice' of the passage the narrator. It is told in the third person from the narrator's point of view. We could write this passage from several points of view.

**1.** Write the first paragraph again from a child's point of view. Use the first person 'I'. The sun has just risen, the day begun and you are still tired ... .

**2.** Now imagine a Sioux is watching the wagon train from the hills. Write the first paragraph, from the Sioux's point of view, using the first person 'I'.

 **E** **Write a diary.**

Imagine you are one of the people on the wagon train. Write your diary entry for the rest of the day. Begin as follows: 'A new hard day had begun ...'

# The Comma

- The comma indicates a brief pause and is used:

**1.** To give additional information about something or someone.

**2.** To separate items in a list, e.g. I saw apples, tomatoes, bread and milk.

**3.** To show a sequence of actions, e.g. Andy made the beds, swept the floors, washed the dishes and cleaned the windows yesterday.

**4.** To separate phrases beginning with the present or past participle, e.g. Striking a match, I peered into a cave.

 **Write these sentences, inserting commas in the correct places.**

**1.** Peter Mary Satish Francis Shanaz and Tom were not in school today.

**2.** Clark Kent did not want his girlfriend Lois Lane to know that he was Superman.

**3.** Anne Brady the hockey team coach had an argument with the referee Mr Cooke.

**4.** Exhausted and soaked we were glad to see the cheerful lights of the hostel.

**5.** The horse suddenly sprang up galloped down the meadow leaped over the stone wall and disappeared into the woods.

**6.** Playing on the beach we did not notice the time go by.

**7.** Thirty days has September April June and November.

**8.** It was midnight before we reached Madrid the capital of Spain.

**9.** The huge tiger suddenly appeared took one look at us and ran.

**10.** I chose the book with the full-colour glossy hardbacked cover.

**11.** Doctor Watt our local doctor was a tall black-haired woman.

**12.** There were numerous jackets jeans and jumpers and shirts on the rail.

**13.** Robbie the clown was able to juggle oranges bananas apples and lemons.

**14.** Areon yawned wiped the sleep from his eyes and combed his fingers through his long fair hair.

**15.** Nesa's eyes were blue her hair as black as a raven.

 **Insert commas and capital letters where necessary in this passage.**

Toby Hopalong australia's most famous kangaroo was worried. he had just spotted a great cloud of thick black smoke on the horizon. realising it was a bushfire he called out to his mate Kiki. "i think we'd better hop it Kiki. there's a fire heading this way – at about 160 kilometres an hour!"

"don't panic toby" said kiki. "i'll round up tessie, skippy and the rest of the kids straight away."

# Nouns

- A noun is a word which tells us the name of a person, place, thing or quality. There are four types of noun:

  **1.** Proper nouns: the names of particular persons, places or things. They always begin with capital letters, e.g. Mary Smith, California, February.

  **2.** Common nouns: the names of things in general, e.g. girl, ball, mountain.

  **3.** Collective nouns: the names of groups of people or things, e.g. herd, flock.

  **4.** Abstract nouns: the names of qualities and feelings, e.g. bravery, loyalty.

 **Rewrite these sentences and underline each noun and say what type of noun it is.**

**1.** Doctor Dalton felt great sadness as she watched the crowd of refugees pouring across the border to Uganda.

**2.** John felt a great sense of happiness as the hot-air balloon soared into the sky.

**3.** Carol said that endurance would be required on the trip to Mount Everest.

 **Make a list of all the nouns you can spot in this picture.**

 **Copy the chart and place the nouns in the correct boxes.**

crew, onion, emptiness, bunch, Joseph, harbour, Jupiter, strength, fish, wall, Monday, army, hatred, danger, Chicago, tribe, excitement, book, gang, Kenya.

| Proper | Common | Collective | Abstract |
|--------|--------|------------|----------|
|        |        |            |          |
|        |        |            |          |

# Dreaming up Stories

One of the greatest gifts we have is that of imagination. Our imagination allows us to think creatively, to dream, to come up with new possibilities, to produce fresh ideas. Even just one word, one object, can be the trigger to fire the imagination into action.

For example, think of one object, a 'ring'. What kind of ring is it – is it golden, an engagement ring or a magical ring? Who owns it – a girl, a young man, an old woman or a wizard? Where is it – on the sea bed, in a jewellery shop? Was it bought, lost, found, inherited or stolen? Already lots of possibilities are coming to mind, any of which could lead to a good story. Of course, if it's to be a good story, there will have to be some problem, or crisis, or conflict concerning this 'ring'. And this problem, crisis or conflict will have to be solved in some way.

 **Create a story idea which would involve each of the following.**

(Try to sum up your story idea in one or two sentences. Remember to take your time, relax and allow your imagination to do the work.)

**1.** A cave

**2.** A key

**3.** A raft

**4.** An old coin

**5.** A map

 **Think up a story idea for each of these characters.**

 **Think up a story for each of these sets of words.**

| Set 1 | Set 2 |
|---|---|
| shark    waterworld | giant tomato    prince |
| monkey    blind girl | fairy    ship |

# Prepositions 1

● A preposition is a word that shows a relationship between things, between nouns and pronouns in the one sentence, e.g. the pen is on the floor; the ball is under the table; we went home after school.

The most common prepositions are:

> about, above, across, after, against, along, among, around, at, before, behind, below, beneath, beside, between, beyond, by, down, during, except, for, from, in, into, near, of, off, on, over, round, since, through, till, to, towards, under, underneath, until, up, upon, with, within, without.

**A** **Put the following prepositions into sentences.**

**1.** until              **2.** beneath
**3.** except            **4.** within

**B** **Copy the sentences, inserting appropriate prepositions.**

**1.** The kitten and puppy slept _____ each other _____ the box.
**2.** Our car skidded _____ the snowstorm.
**3.** I waited _____ seven o'clock and still she had not arrived.
**4.** The weary farmer trudged homewards _____ the fields.
**5.** I went home _____ the match _____ my father.
**6.** The salmon swam in circles _____ the pool.
**7.** We received a parcel _____ Australia.

**C** **Give three prepositions for each of the following.**

**1.** The children hid _____ the bushes.
**2.** The boat sailed _____ the river.

**D** **Write the sentences. Put 'with', 'of' or 'in' in the correct places.**

**1.** I was really surprised when I saw Adam _____ the garden.
**2.** Paul was angry _____ me yesterday.
**3.** I was ashamed _____ myself when I broke the window.

# Tigers on the Brink

The great beast seems to *materialise* out of the dusk – a striped vision of might and mystery. Emerging from a *thicket* in southern India's Nagarahole National Park, the Bengal tigress is hungry and ready to begin another night's hunt. To nourish her 225-kg body, she must kill a deer, a boar or some other big animal every week of her adult life.

But there will be no killing at this moment. After padding along a park road for a mere 90m, the tigress abruptly melts into the brush – here one instant, gone the next. Watching her disappear, Indian biologist Ullas Karanth, of New York's Wildlife Conservation Society, breaks into a knowing smile. "When you see a tiger," he says, "it is always like a dream."

All too soon, dreams may be the only place where tigers roam freely. Already the Nagarahole tigress is not free. If she hunts during the day, she may run into a carload of tourists, cameras clicking. At night, it might be poachers, guns blazing. Once the rulers of their forest home, she and the park's 50 other tigers are now prisoners of human intruders. More than 6,000 Indians live inside the 650-sq-km refuge. And crowding the borders are 250 villages teeming with tens of thousands more people who *covet* not only the animals that the cats need for food but also the tigers (a tiger's *pelt* will fetch a princely sum on the black market). Were it not for the 250 guards on patrol to protect Nagarahole's tigers, none of them would survive for long.

Sadly this *precarious* life is as good as it gets for tigers today. Outside protected areas, Asia's giant cats are a vanishing breed, disappearing faster than any other large mammal with the possible exception of the rhinoceros. Even inside the parks, tigers are coming under threat. No more than 5,000 to 7,500 of the majestic carnivores remain on the planet – a population decline of roughly 95% in this century. Unless something dramatic is done to reverse the trend, tigers will be seen only in captivity, prowling in zoos or performing in circuses. The wild tigers of old will be gone forever, their glory surviving merely in storybooks, on film – and in dreams.

*Time magazine*

**A** **Look up the words in italics in the dictionary section at the back.**

Write down their meaning.

 **B** **Answer the questions.**

**1.** Where exactly did the writer spot the tigress?

**2.** How many tigers remain on the planet today?

**3.** What is a conservation society? Why would it be interested in the tiger?

**4.** Who is Ullas Karanth? Why do you think he said, "When you see a tiger it is always like a dream."

**5.** Name two reasons why tigers are a 'vanishing breed'. Which of these do you think is the more important? Explain why.

**6.** What other animal in the passage is a threatened species? Can you say why this is?

**7.** List three measures that you would take to protect tigers. How might the local people become more involved in the tiger's protection?

 **C** **Make notes on the main points in each paragraph.**

Then summarise the passage in 100 words.

 **D** **Imagine you have been on a trip with Ullas Karanth to see the tiger. Write an article (about 300 words) for a local paper about the plight of the tiger.**

Select five points to include in your article and say what readers could do to help.

Refer to information you have written to help you and remember to think of a suitable headline.

You will need to redraft your work, setting it out appropriately.

# Adjectives

● An adjective is a word which describes or tells us more about a noun. For example, the adjectives 'fierce' or 'shaggy', 'disobedient' or 'loyal' could be used to describe the noun 'dog'. An adjective may be placed before or after the noun, e.g. 'the fierce dog' or 'the dog is fierce'.

 **A** **List seven adjectives from your dictionary (or from the dictionary section in this book).**

happy ...

 **B** **Write as many adjectives as you can to describe these two pictures.**

● Some adjectives can be overused, e.g. 'good', 'nice', 'lovely', 'little', etc.

**C** **Copy the following and choose two interesting adjectives for each.**

The _____ , _____ orange.      A _____ , _____ view.
The _____ , _____ cliff.      A _____ , _____ coat.
The _____ , _____ thief.      A _____ , _____ movie.
The _____ , _____ sea.      A _____ , _____ surgeon.
The _____ , _____ picture.      A _____ , _____ cat.
The _____ , _____ gorilla.      A _____ , _____ skunk.

**D** **Write an adjective that is similar in meaning to each of the following. (Your dictionary may help.)**

| | | |
|---|---|---|
| **1.** timid | **4.** quiet | **7.** polite |
| **2.** upset | **5.** soft | **8.** strict |
| **3.** tired | **6.** serious | **9.** puzzled |

# Writing a Play

A play differs from a novel in many ways.

- Firstly, we need to see a play acted or staged.
- Secondly, the story is revealed through what the characters say.
- Thirdly, a play is written as a script. This records the dialogue or speech of the characters and also the stage directions, which give us simple details about the setting and action.

**A** **Think of another way in which a play differs from a novel and write it down.**

**B** **Read the following. It is an adaption of the beginning of 'Catastrophe' on page 70.**

**Fudge's Turn**

*The family are gathered around the table. It is the baby's birthday. She is covered in sticky cake. Fudge, who is five years old, has been given a book by Grandma. He is staring at it, beaming.*

**Fudge:**       Read to me Grandma.
**Grandma:** Yaaawn.........
**Fudge:**       Go on, Grandma..........plee....ee...ease
*(Tootsie, the baby, bangs her spoon on the table.)*
**Grandma:** Okay, Fudge, where shall we begin?
**Fudge:**       Umm....Uriah......yes, Uriah, I think.

Note how the script has been set out:
- The stage directions are written in italics in the present tense.
- As each character speaks the names (or initials) are given, followed by a colon.
- The dialogue has been developed to suit a play.

**C** **Write your own script for a play, adapted from 'Catastrophe'. Include only two characters and choose one of the following settings:**

1. Tootsie's birthday
2. Tootsie learning to walk
3. Fudge learning to ride his bike
4. Fudge arriving at school on his bike

**D** **Practise your play with a partner and present it to a group.**

# From Story Idea to Plot

● Your imagination will always provide the inspiration for your story. The inspiration is the 'story idea' – something that excites you, interests you, something which you think is worth telling.

● It is important that you are clear about your story idea, that you know exactly what it is. In fact, you should be able to express it in just one sentence. For example, take the story of 'E.T.' (the movie). What is its story idea? In one sentence we might say: 'E.T. is a story of how an alien falls to earth and makes friends with a young boy and his family, who then help it to escape from the clutches of scientists and government agents.'

 **Try to summarise in one sentence the story idea in each of the following.**

1. Cinderella
2. Jack and the Beanstalk
3. Charlie and the Chocolate Factory
4. Jaws
5. Jurassic Park

● The story idea is only the beginning. Now we need a frame or a plan as to how we are going to work this idea out. This plan is called the plot.

● A story with a plot will usually have a start, a middle and an end. It will answer the questions: WHO? WHEN? WHERE? WHAT? HOW? and WHY?

 **Think of a book you have read, your favourite story (or movie, if you prefer). Answer these questions.**

The plot will have dealt with five main areas:
1. THE SETTING: The place where the story was set will have been described. For example, was it in the city, a jungle or the desert? Give some details of the setting.
2. CHARACTERS: The main characters will have been described – both in appearance and in personality. Tell us about the main character(s).
3. THE PROBLEM: In your story there will have been some problem or crisis for the main character(s) to overcome. What was it?
4. THE CLIMAX: How was the problem solved?
5. THE CONCLUSION: What happened after the climax? What did the main character(s) do? How did they feel?

# Sounds – 'scr', 'thr' and 'str'

**A** **Copy the sentences, inserting the correct 'scr' darts.**

> SCREEN   SCRUFFY   SCRIPTURE   SCRUTINISED   SCRUMMAGE
> SCRAMBLED   SCREAMED   SCRIBBLED   SCRUBBED
> SCROLLS   SCRATCHED

1. Alison _____ all over her book and the teacher was annoyed.
2. The explorers discovered ancient _____ in a cave near the Dead Sea.
3. The hotel guests _____ down the fire escape to safety.
4. When we landed in the U.S. a customs officer _____ our passports.
5. The sailors got down on their knees and _____ the deck.
6. The try came following a _____ in front of the French posts.

**B** **Copy these sentences, inserting the correct 'thr' darts.**

> THRONE   THRASHED   THREATENED   THREAD   THROBBED
> THRILL   THRONG
> THRIVED   THROTTLED   THROAT   THRIFT   THRUSH

1. A _____ of fans had gathered outside the hotel, hoping to catch a glimpse of the pop stars.
2. I did not go to choir practice because I had a sore _____ .
3. Crops _____ on the fertile soil of the plain.
4. It _____ to rain and so we hurried home.
5. The pharaoh came to the _____ when he was only eleven years of age.
6. We _____ their team six–nil last season.

**C** **Copy these sentences, inserting the correct 'str' darts.**

> STRAIGHT   STRENUOUS   STROLLED   STRIKE   STRAGGLED
> STRICT   STRAW   STRUCTURE
> STREAKED   STRANDED   STRENGTH   STRETCH

1. A bright comet _____ across the night sky.
2. We collected shells as we _____ along the beach.
3. It was a _____ climb to the top of the mountain.
4. Many holidaymakers were _____ in Spain because of the _____ .
5. The house of _____ that the little pig built was flimsy.
6. The _____ road seemed to _____ forever across the desert.

# Dad the Poacher

"Is that actually what you were doing in Hazell's Wood, Dad? Poaching pheasants?"

"I was practising the art," he said. "The art of poaching."

I was shocked. My own father a thief! This gentle lovely man! I couldn't believe he would go creeping into the woods at night to pinch valuable birds belonging to somebody else.

"Your grandad," he said, "my own dad, was a magnificent and splendiferous poacher. It was he who taught me all about it. I caught the poaching fever from him when I was ten years old and I've never lost it since. Mind you, in those days just about every man in our village was out in the woods at night poaching pheasants. And they did it not only because they loved the sport but because they needed food for their families. When I was a boy, times were bad for a lot of people. There was very little work to be had anywhere, and some families were *literally* starving. Yet a few miles away in a rich man's wood, thousands of pheasants were being fed like kings twice a day. So can you blame my dad for going out occasionally and coming home with a bird or two for the family to eat?"

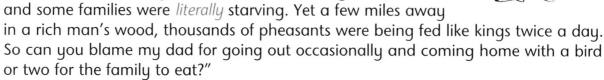

"No," I said. "Of course not. But we're not starving here, Dad."

"You've missed the point, Danny boy! You've missed the whole point! Poaching is such a *fabulous* and exciting sport that once you start doing it, it gets into your blood and you can't give it up! Just imagine," he said, leaping off the bunk and waving his mug of cocoa in the air, "just imagine for a minute that you are all alone up there in the dark wood, and the wood is full of keepers hiding behind trees and the keepers have guns ..."

"Guns!" I gasped. "They don't have guns!"

"All keepers have guns, Danny. It's for the *vermin* mostly, the foxes and stoats and weasels who go after the pheasants. But they'll always take a pot shot at a poacher, too, if they spot him."

"Dad, you're joking."

"Not at all. But they only do it from behind. Only when you're trying to escape. They like to pepper you in the legs at about fifty yards."

"They can't do that!" I cried. "They could go to prison for shooting someone!"

"You could go to prison for poaching," my father said. There was a *glint* and sparkle in his eyes now that I had never seen before.

*Roald Dahl*

**Look up the words in italics in the dictionary section at the back.**

Write down their meaning.

 **Answer these questions.**

    **1.** What is a poacher?

    **2.** How did Danny's dad come to learn about poaching?

    **3.** Why does he do it?

    **4.** Why is it dangerous?

    **5.** Why did people have to poach long ago?

    **6.** In your opinion, do you think poaching is wrong? Explain your answer.

    **7.** Write down what you think a keeper might say about poaching.

 **Explain why.**

Why are capital letters used for 'Hazell's Wood'? Explain why capitals are used for 'Dad' in some sentences and not for 'dad' in other sentences, e.g:

    "Is that actually what you were doing in Hazell's Wood, Dad?"

    "Your grandad," he said, "my own dad, was a magnificent and splendiferous poacher."

 **Read the following:**

**Dad The Poacher**

Danny is shocked to discover that his dad has been poaching in Hazell's Wood. He is questioning him about the incident.

**Danny:**    Is that why you were in Hazell's Wood? Poaching? Poaching, Dad?

**Dad:**    I was practising the art of poaching *(standing up)* – an important difference, Danny.

You will see that the passage has been adapted to suit a play. Note these points about the example:

    **1.** The stage directions are written in italics.

    **2.** As each character speaks the names (or initials) are given, followed by a colon.

    **3.** The writing has been altered (scripted) to suit a play.

Now write your own play script for the whole passage. Think of ideas first and jot them down. Refer to the example and the notes for guidance.

# Singular and Plural

1. For many words (e.g. boy, girl), we add -s to make the plural (boys, girls). In words where it would be difficult to say them with just an -s, we add an -es (e.g. classes, boxes, matches, thrushes).

2. Words ending in -f or -fe, (e.g. half, wife) change to -ves (halves, wives) in the plural. There are some exceptions to this rule ... roof/roofs, cliff/cliffs, chief/chiefs.

3. For words which end in a consonant followed by -y (e.g. city, lady), the -y changes to -i and -es is added (cities, ladies). For words which end in -ey (e.g. donkey, abbey), simply add -s (donkeys, abbeys).

4. If a word ends in -o (e.g. radio, potato) then either -s or -es will be added to make the plural (radios, potatoes). There is no hard and fast rule.

5. Some words have a special form in the plural, e.g. (child – children).

6. A small number of words have the same form in the singular and plural, e.g. (trout, sheep, deer, salmon, cod, plaice, mackerel, grouse).

 **Write the plural of the following words.**

| | | | |
|---|---|---|---|
| **1.** valley | **8.** woman | **15.** witness | **22.** leaf |
| **2.** ring | **9.** army | **16.** passer-by | **23.** lily |
| **3.** watch | **10.** trout | **17.** sky | **24.** swine |
| **4.** daisy | **11.** mouse | **18.** piano | **25.** monkey |
| **5.** thief | **12.** reef | **19.** tomato | **26.** foot |
| **6.** glass | **13.** shelf | **20.** brother-in-law | **27.** ox |
| **7.** hero | **14.** photo | **21.** potato | |

 **Unscramble these nouns which are never used in the singular. The first letter is underlined.**

SSUD          NSGOT          ASTHKN          SSEMLAE

 **Write the following sentences in the singular.**

● Verbs must agree with nouns in the singular and plural, e.g. the girl plays; the girls play.

1. The knives were left on the shelves.
2. The children drink cupfuls of milk.
3. The valleys echo with the songs of the thrushes.
4. The cod were trapped in the trawlers' nets.
5. The foxes play with their cubs in the meadows.

# How to Help Your Spelling

One way you can help yourself become a better speller is to remember the spelling and meaning of common prefixes and suffixes.

*aqua* is a prefix which means water
*aquarium* is a place where live fish are kept.

 **A  Try to work out the rough meaning of these words from the prefix meanings underneath.**

| | | | |
|---|---|---|---|
| aerosol | trio | credible | photogenic |
| submerge | audience | telescope | microchip |
| audible | octagon | tricycle | telecommunications |

aero = air        audi = hear       cred = believe
tri = three       micro = small     oct = eight
photo = light     sub = below       tele = at a distance

Check your answers in a dictionary.

 **B  Do the same with these words but study the suffix meanings.**

| | | |
|---|---|---|
| telescope | software | freedom |
| hardware | include | |

clude = to shut       scope = view
dom = a quality       ware = goods

 **C  Find words beginning with these prefixes.**

ex    hydra    in    port    prim

# Characters

- The character(s) you choose will be at the heart of your plot. It is vital that you know your character well. You can build up your character in three ways:

1. Physical description: What does your character look like? Your choice of adjectives will be important. Is the person tall? Is the hair combed or tousled? Is the complexion fair or dark? Are the shoulders hunched? It is not just about physical features, however. A story should tell us about what kind of person our character is ... perhaps good, evil, trustworthy or shy?

2. Actions: What our character does will tell us more about him/her than anything else. The choice of verbs will be very important.

3. Speech: What does our character say and how does he/she say it?

**A** **Choose two characters (one 'good', the other 'bad') from books you have read (or a movie you have seen). Write what you know about them as characters. What are their names?**

**B** **Write a character sketch about someone you know – maybe someone in your class.**

See if others can guess who it is from your description.

**C** **Write a character sketch for the owners of the objects below.**

**D** **Look carefully at these figures. Write a character sketch on each, using your imagination to fill in the details. Give each person a name. Try to think up a story idea for your characters.**

# Adverbs

- Adverbs are mainly used to tell us more about verbs.
  e.g. Holly watched intently. The soldiers marched slowly. The girls sang happily.
- Most adverbs are formed from adjectives, by adding -ly, or if the adjective already ends in -y, by changing the y to -ily.
- Like adjectives, adverbs, if properly chosen, will greatly improve your writing.

 **Form adverbs from the following adjectives.**

| | | |
|---|---|---|
| **1.** light | **5.** sick | **9.** heavy |
| **2.** careless | **6.** beautiful | **10.** extraordinary |
| **3.** weary | **7.** kind | **11.** greedy |
| **4.** painful | **8.** horrible | **12.** fatal |

 **Rewrite these sentences, choosing a suitable adverb to fill the spaces.**

**1.** Peter cried _____ .

**2.** The hungry wolf howled _____ .

**3.** The sun shone _____ .

**4.** The rain pattered _____ .

**5.** The acrobat leaped _____ .

**6.** The fighter aircraft descended _____ .

**7.** A pair of swans flew _____ .

**8.** The great river flowed _____ .

**9.** A mighty wave crashed _____ .

**10.** The red sports car sped _____ .

**11.** The ridiculous clown laughed _____ .

**12.** The ferocious hurricane struck _____ .

 **Give adverbs that have the opposite meaning.**

| | | |
|---|---|---|
| **1.** bravely | **4.** joyfully | **7.** naturally |
| **2.** correctly | **5.** delicately | **8.** comfortably |
| **3.** fairly | **6.** patiently | **9.** wisely |

# The Circus

While the clowns had been playing about in the ring and on the ring fence, the ring hands had fixed up a trampoline. An old man dressed rather like a ring hand had stood by and supervised.

"Who's that?" Santa whispered to Alexsis.

"That is Mr Frasconi. He is a very great *artiste* of the trampoline. These are his two sons. He teach them and build the act."

The two Frasconi sons were dressed in pink fleshings and a piece of velvet made like leopard skin. The things they did when on the trampoline were breath-taking.

The trampoline might only look rather like a mattress raised off the ground, but it was anything but a mattress to the two brothers. The smaller of the two bounded up and down on it, shooting up as if he would hit the roof, then coming down in amazing twists and *somersaults*. No matter how he came down the bigger brother, who was the bearer, never missed catching him.

"I can't believe they're real," Santa sighed, when at last they finished leaping about and stood bowing on the ground.

After another *reprisal* from the clowns, the ponies trotted in. Alexsis leant forward and watched intently. "I think," he said in a worried voice, "Prissy is not quite well." Peter and Santa gave each other a look. To them the ten ponies looked exactly alike. They suspected Alexsis was showing off.

Maxim Petoff looked grand in the ring. He wore riding things and carried a whip. He never used the whip. He just murmured orders to his ponies and they all obeyed. They had difficult things for a pony to do. They had to divide and trot round in opposite directions. They had to walk round with their forelegs on the ring fence and their *hind* ones in the ring. They had to stand for a moment on their hind legs begging like dogs. When they had finished Maxim stood by the exit and gave each of them something from his pocket as a reward.

Lucille's French poodles were so clever it was almost ridiculous. Three of them did really difficult acrobatic feats. The fourth, who had an enormous sense of humour, was the clown. She tried to do what all the others did and just did it a little wrong. She made the audience rock with laughter.

*Noel Streatfeild*

 **Look up the words in italics in the dictionary section at the back.**

Write down their meaning.

 **Answer these questions.**

**1.** Where did the Frasconi brothers learn their skills?

**2.** Describe what the two Frasconi brothers looked like.

**3.** What impression did they create on Santa?

**4.** Who is Prissy?

**5.** Why did Peter and Santa suspect that Alexsis was 'showing off'?

**6.** Who was Maxim Petoff and why did he look 'grand'?

**7.** What animals were involved in the circus?

**8.** Say whether the passage is fact or fiction. Try to explain how you can tell.

 **Write an article about a visit to the circus.**

It is for a magazine which is running a series on animal welfare (how we look after animals). Write your article as though you are a reporter. (Read some articles in newspapers and magazines to help you.)

Use the information in the passage and consider these points:

**1.** Whether or not it is right to make animals perform tricks.

**2.** Whether or not animals should be made to wear clothes.

**3.** What the general public thinks about animal welfare.

When you have written your first draft consider these points:

**4.** Plan how you will lay out the article (for example, in columns).

**5.** Think of a suitable headline; one which sums up the article.

**6.** Include a quotation from the article which would be set in bold letters.

Now redraft your article, setting it out properly.

 **Imagine that you are the next act in this circus.**

Write about yourself, how you are dressed and what you do. How do you feel – excited, nervous, terrified or happy?

# Connectives: Meaning and Spelling

Connectives, like prepositions, connect different parts of a sentence.
They can also connect one sentence with another.

*Warren spent all his money. **Therefore**, he couldn't buy presents for his relatives.*

**Therefore** helps to tell us why Warren couldn't buy presents.
It helps to give us a reason.

To remember how to spell **therefore**, split the word into two: **there  fore**.

 **Write down the connectives which give a reason or follow on, logically, in the sentences below. (There may be more than one in a sentence.)**

1. Julie bought the tickets early so she would not have to queue.
2. Warren's aunt was waiting at the station. However, she was on the wrong platform and as a result she missed him.
3. Julie did not arrive on time because she caught the wrong train.
4. Uncle Jack waited an hour for Julie. In addition he phoned her mother because he became increasingly worried.
5. Warren decided he would have to make his own way to Valley Farm, despite his concerns.
6. Julie and Warren arrived at the farm at the same time. Consequently, they were able to laugh about their mistakes.
7. Uncle Jack and Aunt Molly arrived home flustered and irritated. Nevertheless, they put on cheerful faces when they found Julie and Warren.

 **Split the more difficult connectives into separate words or syllables to help you remember the spelling.**

# Prepositions 2

You may remember that prepositions are words or groups of words that show a relationship between things in one sentence.

The cat left her toy mouse **by** the chair.
**by** tells where the mouse is or the position of the mouse.

 **Finish these sentences using a suitable preposition telling you the position of something.**

**1.** Dave collected the bag which was lying ...
**2.** Davinia sped quickly ...
**3.** Ray laid his guitar ...
**4.** Joy climbed ...
**5.** The snail crawled ...

 **Use the following prepositions in three sentences.**

**1.** nearby, above       **2.** against, in front of       **3.** among, beside

Other words, such as adverbs, can also connect parts of a sentence.
The words firstly, secondly, thirdly, tell you the order or sequence of something.

 **Write one sentence using: firstly, secondly, thirdly.**

Remember to use the correct punctuation.

 **Write out a) and b) replacing the words in bold with other prepositions.**

**a)** He went to the cinema **on** his own.
**b)** He went **over** the road.

You can replace other words but you must not change the meaning of the sentence.

 **Complete these sentences with two prepositions to show different meanings.**

**1.** He is completely _____ the control of the Mountain King.
**2.** The river passed slowly _____ the ancient stone bridge.

# Fighting the Fire Demon

Trees explode into an inferno; balls of fire leap from tree top to tree top; the wind whips inwards to refuel the *holocaust* of fire and smoke. Close up, a forest fire is a terrifying spectacle.

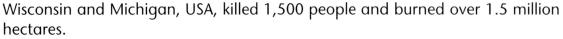

But it is a scene repeated thousands of times a year in *temperate* forests around the world, most dramatically in the wilderness areas of California and the bushlands of Southern Australia. These areas fall easy prey to a dropped match, sunlight *amplified* through a discarded bottle, or a lightning-bolt. In Australia, the heat of a fire can vaporise eucalyptus oil, igniting whole trees in gaseous explosions.

The destruction can be massive. In 1949, France lost 155,800 hectares of forest in 350 fires. In 1971, fires in Wisconsin and Michigan, USA, killed 1,500 people and burned over 1.5 million hectares.

Flames can spread through tinder-dry bush at speeds of over 114 km/h. Occasionally the combustion causes a fire whirlwind, a chimney of hot air supplied by inrushing winds that can uproot trees and shoot them into the air, starting new fires hundreds of metres away.

To combat a blaze, firefighters use a combination of two main strategies: cooling and containment. *Dousing* a fire with water cools it, breaks up burning material, and when turned into steam it reduces the amount of oxygen in the air to feed the fire. But water by itself may not be enough. The fires can spread beneath mosses and lichens, and can survive inside hummocks and old stumps to break out again days later. To reduce these 'hot spots', chemicals are mixed with the water to help it penetrate. And dyes may be added to show which areas of forest have been treated.

Ground crews may use bulldozers to create firebreaks to contain the blaze, while air tankers 'bomb' the fire with thousands of litres of water and chemicals.

But some bushfires get so out of control that there is a limit to what firefighters can do about them. They simply have to wait for the fire to burn itself out. As Australian Fire Brigade Captain, Graham Simpson, remarked, "A major bushfire is a *cataclysm* creating its own wind and weather, a demon with a mind of its own."

**A** **Look up the words in italics in the dictionary section at the back.**

Write down their meaning.

 **B** **Answer these questions.**

1. How are bushfires caused?
2. Give two reasons why these forest fires spread rapidly.
3. How might it happen that a new fire can suddenly break out well away from the inferno?
4. What two main strategies are used by firefighters to overcome the blaze? Explain what these mean.
5. What is a firebreak?
6. When the flames have been put out firefighters must still be on guard. Explain why.
7. What was the average amount of forest hectares lost per fire in France back in 1949?
8. There have been an increasing number of similar fires throughout the world. Can you say why? If not, find out, using ICT.

 **C** **Make two columns: Fact and Opinion.**

Decide in which column the following statements belong and write down the number.

1. Trees explode into an inferno.
2. Close up, a forest fire is a terrifying spectacle.
3. In 1949, France lost 155,800 hectares of forest in 350 fires.
4. A major bushfire is a ... demon with a mind of its own.
5. ... fires in Wisconsin and Michigan, USA, killed 1,500 people ...
6. Flames can spread through tinder-dry bush at speeds of over 114 km/h.
7. To reduce these 'hot spots', chemicals are mixed with the water to help it penetrate.

Choose two examples from above, one fact and one opinion, and explain why you have classified them in this way.

# Dashes, Brackets and Commas

- A dash is like a colon. It means a pause, but it is sharper and separates extra information in a sentence.

  *She was happy to receive the invitation – we think so, anyway – and thanked the family for considering her.*

 **Write out these sentences putting the dashes in the correct place.**

1. It was one of the best shows at least during the last few months that we have seen.
2. Joe returned the box of tools he made sure nothing was missing on Monday morning.
3. I think she went that way though I can't say for certain about half an hour ago.

- Brackets also separate information but they are slightly different from dashes. They allow you to carry on reading more easily.

  *The loft (also called the attic) is an important feature of these new houses.*

 **Write out these sentences putting in the brackets correctly.**

1. The tickets only £7 each were available for the evening performance.
2. Tomorrow Monday is the first day of the holiday and we are all going to the beach!
3. He ran up the stairs three steps at a time to find the letter he had received that morning.

- Sometimes people use commas instead of brackets.

 **The commas have been put in the wrong places in these sentences. Write them out correctly.**

1. The two boys, both received joint first, prize £100 and stepped up to receive it.
2. The journey should take no more than four hours or just over providing there isn't too, much, traffic.
3. If, we put all, the toys including Samira's games in that cupboard we should have enough space.

# Changes Over Time

Language does not stay the same. It gets used differently by different generations and in different periods of history. For example, there are many English words that we no longer use. However, we can work out what many of these words mean because they are similar to the modern words that have replaced them.

Read these words from William Shakespeare's *A Midsummer Night's Dream*.

**Oberon:**     Seest thou this ... ?

**It means:**    Do you see this ... ?

 **Read the following conversation. Note all the words that sound strange and make you laugh.**

"Cometh here!" yelled Wayne at the top of his voice.
"Whist!" replied Darren, who was busy.
Wayne spoke again, quietly, this time, "List, Darren, seest thou yonder?"
Darren, becoming curious, turned thither and saw ...

Write out the passage replacing the old-fashioned words with modern ones. Check in a dictionary if you cannot guess what the words are.

 **Find out what these words mean and write down the modern equivalent.**

| prithee | whither | writ | wherefore | hadst | |
| nay | dost | quoth | is't | 'twas | whithersoever |

Now finish the dialogue between Wayne and Darren using some old-fashioned words.

 **There are many other, more recent, words that we no longer use or may use occasionally. Try to guess what these words mean and write them down.**

frock        wireless        drawing room        airboat

# New Words

As the world around us changes and new ideas develop, so our language changes to cope with these new ideas.

For example a car once meant a cart or wagon, now it refers to a motor car.

Remember:
- Words can shift in meaning.
- Words can develop more than one meaning.
- New words can appear.

 **Write down your answer to this question.**

Why do you think people did not use the word aeroplane 200 years ago?

 **Explain what these expressions mean.**

fab     well-bad     gross     rad     wicked

 **Think of two meanings for these words.**

| | | | | |
|---|---|---|---|---|
| mouse | monitor | hardware | floppy | |
| web | menu | window | screen | scroll |

Use a dictionary if you need to.

What do the words above have in common? Write down your answer.

 **Find other words for these or explain their meanings.**

| | | | | |
|---|---|---|---|---|
| trainers | wheelie | freebie | Frisbee | denims |
| Hoover | platforms | skateboard | leggings | |

Why might some of these words have changed in ten years time?

# Colons and Semicolons

A colon is two dots like this :
We often use the colon when we want to give instructions, show something or list information. It is like a long break or pause. Look at the following:
*Yesterday I bought: three pairs of socks, a red hat, a comic and a bunch of bananas!*
Notice where the commas go.

 **Put the colon and where necessary, commas, in the right places in these sentences.**

1. Nina had several presents to buy a birthday present for Rachel an anniversary present for Aunt Betty and Uncle Ron and a special present for her dad.
2. The instructions began

   a) remove all parts from box and set out accordingly.
3. She had packed her case in a hurry and forgot many items a pair of shoes a toothbrush a jumper her book and worst of all her glasses.

 **Finish the dialogue between Fred and the mongrel dog.**

We also use colons when we want to write a dialogue or a play script. Read the following:
*Fred has a stall every Saturday at the local market. Sometimes he has unusual customers.*

**Fred:**          Can I help you, Sir?
**Mongrel Dog:**   Woof, can I have ...

 **How many times has the colon been used to give you instructions and information on this page?**

The semicolon is used to show that two events or ideas are closely linked. The second part of the sentence usually gives extra information about the first, like this:
*They threw a party when they moved into their new home; it was a very special occasion.*

 **Turn the following pairs of sentences into one, using a semicolon.**

1. It was a clear, cold night. The moon and stars could be seen easily.
2. Maria smiled at her small brother. She could be very good-natured, sometimes.
3. Daniel had forgotten his money again. It was the third time this week.

# Aunt Agatha and the New Lodger

Aunt Agatha, like her house, was tall, old and narrow. On a good day, when she swept her hair up into swirls (like the ice cream in an ice cream cornet) and put on her best dress, she could look quite elegant. On a bad day, like today, she looked taller, older and narrower than ever before. Sometimes Henry looked at the photographs of Aunt Agatha that stood on top of the piano in their *tarnished* silver frames and wondered what had happened to her. Here she was as a bride, all plump and pretty and smiling. And here she was with a baby in her arms, looking gentle and happy.

Henry had never seen Aunt Agatha looking either. He thought that somehow or other Aunt Agatha had wintered. The plumpness, the prettiness, the gentleness and happiness had dropped off her like leaves at the end of summer and left her *gaunt* and *stark* as a winter tree.

Henry knew at once that Aunt Agatha had had a bad day because of the angry angle of the pencil she kept behind her ear to do her *accounts*. It looked more like an arrow than a pencil. Aunt Agatha sat at the kitchen table with her sharp eyes and pointed nose directed at a large cheery-faced man with ginger whiskers, a tartan waistcoat and a black beret.

1.8 metres at least, thought Henry, and not a hope of fitting into the attic. Ginger Whiskers was smiling hopefully at Aunt Agatha. Aunt Agatha looked as *grim* as a funeral.

"Tell me something about your diet," said Aunt Agatha. Ginger Whiskers looked cheerier than ever. He grinned at Henry.

"Well now, Miss Agatha, I'm pleased to tell you that I've a very healthy appetite and that I'm not a fussy man. No, not me. I'll eat anything I'm given."

Which wouldn't be very much, thought Henry.

"I see," said Aunt Agatha frostily. She pulled the pencil out from behind her ear. Henry, standing behind her, saw her write down 'Greedy'. He could also see that there was a long list of names in Aunt Agatha's notebook, all of them crossed out and given a final judgement like 'too tall', 'too fat', 'too talkative', 'too cheerful'.

"Henry!" said Aunt Agatha, turning sharply. "You can start peeling potatoes for supper." Henry dumped his bag in the corner and went over to the sink ... Aunt Agatha carried on with her questions. She reminded Henry of detectives he'd seen on television questioning criminals.

*Diana Hendry*

38

**Look up the words in italics in the dictionary section at the back.**

Write down their meaning.

 **Answer these questions.**

1. Write one sentence in your own words to say how Aunt Agatha is described in the passage.
2. How does Henry think Aunt Agatha used to be?
3. What does the description, 'Aunt Agatha had wintered' mean?
4. Who is 'Ginger Whiskers'?
5. What does Henry think Ginger Whiskers' chances are of pleasing Aunt Agatha? How can you tell?
6. In what way does Ginger Whiskers contrast with Aunt Agatha?
7. What does Henry mean when he thinks that Aunt Agatha reminds him 'of detectives he'd seen on television questioning criminals'?
8. If Henry were to judge Aunt Agatha as she judges others, what do you think he would write in his notebook?
9. Find four similes in the passage and say what they describe.

 **Think about Aunt Agatha's personality.**

Write down six questions she would ask Ginger Whiskers.

 **Write a description which is divided into two parts.**

In the first part Aunt Agatha is describing herself when she was a young woman but, unlike the description in the passage, she sees herself as shy and unconfident.

In the second part, she is describing her life now. Again, her view of herself is different from the description in the passage. She sees herself as much more in command of her life, as 'elegant', with 'her hair swept up in swirls'.

Write in the first person, 'I'.

# Miyax, Alone

By the yellow-green light of the low noon sun Miyax could see that she had camped on the edge of the wintering grounds of the caribou. Their many *gleaming* antlers formed a forest on the horizon. Such a herd would certainly attract her pack. She crawled out of bed and saw that she had pitched her tent in a tiny forest about three inches high. Her heart pounded excitedly, for she had not seen one of these willow *groves* since Nunivak. She was making progress, for they grew, not near Barrow, but in slightly warmer and wetter lands near the coast. She smelled the air in the hope that it bore the salty *odour* of the ocean, but it smelled only of the cold.

The dawn cracked and hummed and the snow was so fine that it floated above the ground when a breeze stirred. Not a bird passed overhead. The buntings, long-spurs, and terns were gone from the top of the world.

A willow ptarmigan, the chicken of the *tundra*, clucked behind her and whistled softly as it hunted seeds. The Arctic Circle had been returned to its permanent bird resident, the hardy ptarmigan. The millions of voices of summer had died down to one *plaintive* note.

Aha, ahahahahahaha! Miyax sat up, wondering what that was. Creeping halfway out of her bag, she peered into the sky to see a great brown bird manoeuvre its wings and speed west.

"A skua!" She was closer to the ocean than she thought, for the skua is a bird of the coastal waters of the Arctic. As her eyes followed it, they came to rest on an oil drum, the signpost of American civilisation in the North. How excited she would have been to see this a month ago; now she was not so sure. She had her ulo and needles, her sled and her tent, and the world of her ancestors. And she liked the simplicity of that world. It was easy to understand. Out here she understood how she fitted into the *scheme* of the moon and stars and the constant rise and fall of life on earth. Even the snow was part of her, she melted and drank it.

Amaroq barked. He sounded as if he was no more than a quarter of a mile away.

"Ow, ooo," she called. Nails answered, and then the whole pack howled briefly.

"I'm over here!" she shouted joyously, jumping up and down. "Here by the lake." She paused. "You know that. You know everything about me."

*Jean Craighead George*

**Look up the words in italics in the dictionary section at the back.**

Write down their meaning.

 **Answer the questions.**

   **1.** Where is the story set?
   **2.** Why might wolves be attracted to this location?
   **3.** Why was Miyax glad to come across the willow grove?
   **4.** Why were there so few birds in the area?
   **5.** What bird had remained?
   **6.** What other evidence was there that Miyax was approaching the sea?
   **7.** How can you tell Miyax was in touch with nature?
   **8.** Why was she delighted to hear the howling of wolves?
   **9.** Try to suggest why Miyax was alone.

 **Consider the character of Miyax and answer these questions.**

   **1.** What does the following quotation tell you about Miyax? 'Out here she understood how she fitted into the scheme of the moon and stars and the constant rise and fall of life on earth.'
   **2.** Who is Amaroq? Why does he understand Miyax?
   **3.** Write a short character study of her. Refer to the passage to help you.

 **Description.**

There are vivid descriptions in the passage. For instance, 'The dawn cracked and hummed', refers to the ice cracking and making noises as the sun rises.
   **1.** Explain what these refer to:
      **a)** 'By the yellow-green light of the low noon sun'
      **b)** 'The millions of voices of summer'
   **2.** Write short descriptions of the following. Try to write in the style of the passage:
      **a)** a skua flying across the snow          **b)** a wolf meeting Miyax
      **c)** the moon and stars over the Arctic
   **3.** Read the passage again. Write a sequel to it in which Miyax has a dream about her ancestors. Use your own descriptions.

# More About Paragraphs

- All the sentences in a paragraph deal with the same main idea or action.
- A new paragraph will come about when we shift to a new idea, or a new piece of the action, when new characters appear, or when some time has elapsed in the story. How the paragraphs are organised, one after the other, is very important. As far as possible try to make your paragraphs fit together so that they appear to blend in a natural way.

 **Let us look at the middle section of a story. Middle paragraphs usually deal with a problem or conflict of some sort. Write two paragraphs about the following scene.**

 **Will our space heroes survive and fight their way to safety? We reach the climax of the story. Write a third paragraph based on the picture below.**

# Dobbin

**1**

The old horse, Dobbin
Out at grass
Turns his tail
To the winds that pass
And stares at the white road
Winding down
Through the dwindling fields
To the distant town.

**2**

He hears in the distance
A snip-snap trot
He sees his Master
a small dark dot
Riding away
On a new smart mare
That came last month
From Pulborough Fair.

**3**

Dobbin remembers
As horses may
How often he trotted
That ringing way.
His coat is ragged
And blown awry
He drops his head
And knows not why.

**4**

Something has happened
Something has gone
The world is changing
His work is done.
But his old heart aches
With a heavier load
As he stands and wonders
And he stares at the road.

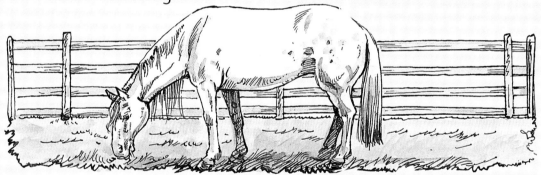

 **Answer these questions.**

1. Do you like this poem? What makes it a good poem?

2. Why is Dobbin so downhearted?

3. What feelings does this poem arouse in you? How does the poet elicit (draw out) our sympathy for Dobbin?

4. Compare Dobbin's appearance to that of the new horse.

5. In what way is the fourth verse different from the rest?

6. Sometimes a poet uses the sounds of words in a way that will imitate the real sounds of the object in question. This is called onomatopoeia. Find one example of this in the poem.

7. What happy memories might Dobbin recall of the 'good old days'?

8. Do you think horses have 'feelings' in the way this poem describes?

# Comparison of Adjectives

- When adjectives are used to compare one thing with another they change their form, e.g. tall – taller – tallest.

  **1.** 'Anne is tall.' Where no comparison is being made, the adjective is said to be in the positive degree.

  **2.** 'Anne is taller than Grace.' In this example, a comparison is being made between two persons. The comparative degree of the adjective is used.

  **3.** 'Anne is the tallest in the class.' Here more than two are being compared and the adjective is said to be in the superlative degree.

- As a general rule, single-syllable adjectives form the comparative and superlative by adding -r or -er, and -st or -est respectively.

 **A  Copy and complete this table.**

| POSITIVE | COMPARATIVE | SUPERLATIVE |
|---|---|---|
| white | whiter | whitest |
| wise | | |
| quick | | |
| noble | | |
| new | | |
| long | | |
| fast | | |
| brave | | |

- Some two-syllable words, e.g. lucky, dirty, etc. take on the comparative and superlative forms in a similar way to the above cases, e.g. lucky – luckier – luckiest. But as a general rule, for adjectives of two or more syllables, the comparative is made by using 'more' and the superlative by using 'most' with the positive, e.g. beautiful – more beautiful – most beautiful.

**B  Copy and complete this table.**

| POSITIVE | COMPARATIVE | SUPERLATIVE |
|---|---|---|
| lovely | lovelier | loveliest |
| generous | | |
| distant | | |
| reasonable | | |
| merry | | |
| efficient | | |
| patient | | |

● The comparison of certain adjectives is irregular, e.g. good – better – best.

 **Copy and complete this table.**

| POSITIVE | COMPARATIVE | SUPERLATIVE |
|---|---|---|
| bad | _ _ _ s _ | _ _ _ _ t |
| little | _ _ s _ | _ _ a _ _ |
| far | _ u _ _ _ _ | _ u _ _ _ _ _ |
| many | _ _ r _ | _ _ _ t |
| up | _ _ _ _ r | _ _ _ _ _ most |
| old | older | oldest |
| old | e _ _ _ r* | e _ _ _ _ t |

\* used only when comparing persons in the same family (e.g. My e_ _ _ _ r brother is fifteen.)

 **Write a sentence containing the superlative form of an adjective for each of the following.**

**1.** The Nile          The Nile is the longest river in the world.

**2.** Mount Everest

**3.** China

**4.** Einstein

**5.** The blue whale

**6.** A diamond

**E** **Make the correct choice of word for each of these sentences. Write out the correct sentence.**

**1.** That oak tree is the *(oldest, eldest)* living thing in this country.

**2.** Who is *(taller, tallest)*, Paul or Joe?

**3.** My stamp collection is *(better, best)* than yours.

**4.** Which is the *(better, best)* international side – Brazil, Italy or Germany?

**5.** Paste the pictures on the *(smoother, smoothest)* side of the page.

**6.** It was obvious that Margaret was the *(more, most)* determined of the eight runners in the final.

**7.** It would be hard to find a *(more nicer, nicer)* spot in the world than this green valley.

**8.** Mirror, mirror, tell me true, who is the *(fairer, fairest)* of the two?

# Using a Dictionary

- A dictionary is used for finding out the meaning of a word, and for checking the correct spelling of a word. A dictionary will also tell us whether a word is a noun, an adjective, a verb or an adverb.

- Words in a dictionary are always arranged in alphabetical order. If all the words begin with the same letter, then we look at the alphabetical order of the second letter and so on.

 **Arrange these groups of words in alphabetical order.**

1. scent, bailiff, rogue, umpire, candid, yearn, timid, frieze
2. feeble, fumble, favourite, froth, forlorn, flinch, fiend
3. hundred, hunt, hurricane, humble, human, hum, humbug, hurl
4. scribble, scruple, scream, scrumptious, scrutiny, scrawl, scree
5. inherit, inside, image, improve, illness, instant
6. empty, enter, enjoy, envy, escape, election
7. shin, shield, smart, skittle, skunk, ship, sew

 **Write down the first seven words you would expect to find in your dictionary under the letter 't'.**

table ...

 **Write down the meaning of the following words from a dictionary.**

shrapnel          reminisce

 **Open any page of your dictionary, write down all the nouns you find.**

Put them into sentences.

 **Open any page of your dictionary. Can you put four of the words you find there into one sentence?**

e.g. I shuddered when I was shown the shrimp that had shrunk.

# Mnemonics

A mnemonic (said nem-on-ic) is a useful spelling aid. It can help you remember words you are unsure of. You make up a word for each letter, like this:

To spell *apple* you could say to yourself: **a**ll **p**ink **p**arrots **l**ay **e**ggs

You may wish to make up a mnemonic for the part of the word you get wrong. For example, *rember* should be spelled *re**mem**ber*, so you could say to yourself **m**y **e**lastic **m**ango or **m**any **e**legant **m**onsters.

You could also try to remember smaller words within longer more difficult words:

**name** in tournament          **all** in gallery

 **A**  **Work out these mnemonics.**

   **1.** kippers never eat worms
   **2.** little owls spy eels
   **3.** please rattle each silly sausage
   **4.** hippos expect instant rice
   **5.** think how owls understand great hamsters
   **6.** we employ ants readily in new gardens
   **7.** all bears stock each new chicken egg

 **B**  **Find smaller words in these longer words and write them out. (Do not re-arrange the letters.)**

situation      together      narrative      awareness
personally     impact        vocabulary

Now make up mnemonics for the words you have found.

 **C**  **Make up mnemonics for these words using the first letter of each word.**

twist      does      world      again      cough

# Fighting the Fire

1. What has happened here?
2. Where is the fire located? Choose words carefully to describe the fire. Describe the damage done by it.
3. If the cause of the fire was accidental, how do you think it happened? If the cause was malicious, who do you imagine might have started it? How? Why? When?
4. Look at the members of the fire brigade. What are they doing? Have they just arrived on the scene? Are they in a state of high alert? Are they talking? What might they be saying to each other? What will they do next?
5. Give a description of the uniform worn by the firefighter on the right-hand side. What do you think the helmet is made of? Why is it bright yellow in colour?
6. Talk about the passer-by. Describe him. Give him a name. Where does he live? Where is he going? What is going through his mind as he watches the flames?
7. Besides the actual fire, what, in your opinion, is the most striking visual image in the photograph?
8. Who might suffer as a result of this fire? What, in your opinion, is the best way to prevent fires like this one?

# Proverbs

- A proverb is a traditional saying which offers advice or presents a moral.

 **A** **Complete these well-known proverbs. What does each one mean?**

**1.** A bird in the hand is worth

**2.** Better late than

**3.** Birds of a feather

**4.** A leopard does not change

**5.** Too many cooks spoil

**6.** Actions speak louder

**7.** The early bird

**8.** Don't count your chickens

 **B** **Match the proverb with its meaning.**

**1.** Let sleeping dogs lie.

**2.** Rome was not built in a day.

**3.** Look before you leap.

**4.** Cut your coat according to your cloth.

**5.** Half a loaf is better than none.

**6.** Every cloud has a silver lining.

**7.** Better to wear out than to rust out.

**a.** Even when things are gloomy, there's always some hope.

**b.** To have something is better than to have nothing at all.

**c.** It takes time to achieve great things.

**d.** Don't do anything suddenly or without advice.

**e.** Where there has been trouble before it's better not to stir it up.

**f.** Work, even though it may be hard, is better than being idle.

**g.** Whatever action you take should suit your circumstances or resources.

**C** **Write in your own words what you think these proverbs mean.**

Don't put all your eggs in one basket.
A stitch in time saves nine.
Once bitten, twice shy.
When the cat's away the mice will play.
The more haste, the less speed.
Beauty is only skin deep.

# Popping to the Movies for Cholesterol by the Bucketful

The scariest thing at the movies these days may not be what's on the screen but what's in your lap. That's the message from a food watchdog group in the U.S. which has reviewed the fat content of cinema popcorn and given it the thumbs down.

The delicious-smelling popcorn sold in most U.S. cinemas – as American as baseball and apple pie – is a *nutritional* disaster, according to the Centre for Science and Public Interest in Washington.

A medium-sized butter-flavoured popcorn, they found, contains as much fat as a bacon and egg breakfast, a Big Mac, a large chips, and a steak dinner – combined.

Even without the melted butter, a medium popcorn sold in some cinemas contains more than double the *artery*-clogging saturated fat found in a Big Mac and large french fries.

Mind you, in American picture houses popcorn is sold in bucket-sized cartons and a 'medium-sized' container holds about 25 handfuls. A 'large' 45-handful carton at Cineplex Odeon or United Artists cinemas contains a whopping 1,642 *calories* and as much saturated fat as 15 hot dogs. A 'small' popcorn without butter still contains the maximum amount of saturated fat the U.S. health authorities recommend for a single day.

Popcorn can be made in three ways – with coconut oil, coconut oil with topping, or canola shortening. The chief villain is the sweet-smelling coconut oil which is 86 per cent saturated. Seven out of ten cinemas still 'pop' the corn in coconut oil. By contrast, supermarket popcorn, and air-popped popcorn like that made at home, makes for a safe, wholesome, high-fibre snack.

"We're pleased to have this information," Mr William Kartozian, president of the National Association of Theatre-Owners, said. But he pointed out that the average person only goes to the cinema six times a year.

"Going to the cinema and settling in for popcorn, a soft drink and a candy bar – it's one of life's small *indulgences*," he said.

But wait. The Centre for Science and Public Interest has been looking at candy bars and soft drinks too. 'Just keep in mind that a whole box or a bar of some of these candies has unbelievable amounts of sugar,' its report says.

Listing well-known bars including Whoppers and KitKat, it goes on: 'If you eat a whole over-sized theatre-candy box or bar, you'll get close to a day's allowance of saturated fat.'

As for the soft drink, it's almost as lethal a weapon as popcorn. A 32-ounce medium (bucket-size) Coke-Classic 'slaps you with 300 calories and 21 teaspoons of sugar,' the report says.

Conor O' Clery for *The Irish Times*

 **Look up the words in italics in the dictionary section at the back.**

Write down their meaning.

 **Answer these questions.**

1. What does the writer say is the scariest thing at the movies?
2. Explain what a food 'watchdog' is. Which is the one mentioned here?
3. What does the expression 'as American as baseball and apple pie' mean?
4. What wholesome 'high-fibre snack' is mentioned in the passage? How is it different from cinema popcorn?
5. Who is Mr William Kartozian? Make a comment on his remark: "We're pleased to have this information."
6. What else is mentioned in the passage that is bad for our health? Give two examples.
7. Why has the writer chosen this title for his article? How is it 'a play on words'?

 **What evidence (proof) does the journalist refer to when he is making his points?**

Find three examples.

 **Creating an article.**

Look carefully at how the journalist makes the points in his article and how one paragraph leads to another. For example: In paragraph one he introduces the topic 'cinema popcorn ... gets the thumbs down'. This leads to paragraph two which restates the point and explains why: it is 'a nutritional disaster'.

1. Find key words in each paragraph or write short notes of your own which summarise the main points.
2. Show how one paragraph leads to another or shifts to a new point. In particular explain why the writer opens paragraph eight with 'But wait ... '
3. How do you think the writer views the report from the Centre for Science and Public Interest? (Think carefully.)

 **There are people who like to eat food which is not good for them. Think of three points they could make to persuade people to ignore the article.**

# Tartary

If I were Lord of Tartary,
Myself, and me alone,
My bed should be of ivory,
Of beaten gold my throne;
And in my court should peacocks flaunt,
And in my forests tigers haunt,
And in my pools great fishes slant
Their fins athwart the sun.

If I were Lord of Tartary,
Trumpeters every day
To all my meals should summon me,
And in my courtyards bray;
And in the evening lamps should shine,
Yellow as honey, red as wine,
While harp and flute and mandoline
Made music sweet and gay.

If I were Lord of Tartary,
I'd wear a robe of beads,
White, and gold, and green they'd be –
And small and thick as seeds;
And ere should wane the morning star,
I'd don my robe and scimitar,
And zebras seven should draw my car
Through Tartary's dark glades.

Lord of the fruits of Tartary,
Her rivers silver-pale!
Lord of the hills of Tartary,
Glen, thicket, wood and dale!
Her flashing stars, her scented breeze,
Her trembling lakes, like foamless seas,
Her bird-delighting citron-trees,
In every purple vale!

*Walter De La Mare*

**Answer these questions.**

    **1.** Describe the land of Tartary. Would you like to visit there?

    **2.** Why do you think the poet wants to be like the Lord of Tartary?

 **Make five headings of the senses in your book: Sight, Sound, Smell, Taste, Touch.**

Write the words which appeal to each sense in the correct column.

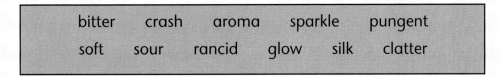

| bitter | crash | aroma | sparkle | pungent |
| soft | sour | rancid | glow | silk | clatter |

Now find words in the poem that appeal to the five senses and add them to the correct column.

 **Look at the rhythm.**

    **1.** How many syllables are in the first line? Tap them out with your hand and write them down.

    **2.** Do the same with all the other lines in the first verse. What pattern do you get?

    **3.** This rhythm is repeated throughout the poem. What does it remind you of? (Think of what the Lord of Tartary is like.)

    **4.** Now write down which line is repeated in the poem.

    **5.** Read the poem to yourself again. Try to explain more fully how repeating the line and the rhythm of the poem adds to its appeal.

 **In the poem some words have been put together to make new words.**

bird-delighting       citron-trees

Think of some words like this of your own to describe an imaginary land. If you wish you can combine words from the poem or use words from B, above.

 **Write a poem in the same style for your imaginary land.**

53

# Active and Passive

We can write some sentences in different ways and still say the same thing.
*Children like cartoons.*
This is called the active because we are saying directly that Children like ...

We can write this another way by changing the words around and also the verb:
Cartoons are liked by children.
This is called the **passive** because we shift **what is liked** to the beginning of the sentence: *Cartoons are liked ...*

Read this further example:
*All pigs love mud. Mud is loved by all pigs.*

 **Change these sentences from the active to the passive.**

   **1.** The pot-bellied pigs loved this sty.
   **2.** Keith put the fish in the new aquarium.
   **3.** The pigeons ate all the bread.
   **4.** The dog chewed the glove to shreds.

 **Change these sentences from the passive to the active.**

   **1.** Its young were protected by the gorilla.
   **2.** The juiciest leaves were munched by the giraffe.
   **3.** The deer was stalked across the plains by the lion.
   **4.** The banana was stolen from the boy by the monkey.

Now read the following.
*We kept the chicks in an incubator.* **(active)**
*The chicks were kept in an incubator by us.* **(passive)**
*The chicks were kept in an incubator.* **(passive)**

You will see that sometimes we choose not to write the by-phrase.

**Change the following leaving out the by-phrase.**

   **1.** They carried the puppies to the car.
   **2.** He fed the geese this afternoon.
   **3.** She bought the kitten a toy.
   **4.** We gave the guinea pig some clean straw.
   **5.** The starlings built a nest in the roof.

# Revising Work on Complex Sentences

 **Write out the main clause in these sentences, like this.**

**We flew together** in the balloon.
1. I will clean my bike before we leave.
2. We will buy some chocolates when we arrive.
3. On the way we collected the presents.

 **Finish these sentences by writing them out with a main clause, like this.**

**He caught the child** as she ran into the road.
1. Before I dive into the pool ...
2. ... with his caravan in good shape.
3. If you decide to go ...
4. ... as they swim across the oceans.

 **Turn the following pairs of sentences into complex sentences, like this.**

He rescued the kitten. He climbed the tree. He stretched his arm.
He rescued the kitten by climbing the tree and stretching his arm.

Use a range of connectives.
1. The dog yapped. It leapt in the air. It was very excited.
2. We were scared out of our wits. We saw the ghost. It was deathly white.
3. Pip and Anna were walking along. They found a purse. It had a gold clasp.

**D** **Decide where the commas go and write out the sentences.**

1. The game which was due to be played at 3pm was late starting.
2. Jo had bought new trainers made with special soles for the sports day.
3. Phil who was very nervous accepted the gold cup and smiled.
4. Polly stepped into the water which was clear and blue to begin the race.

# At Home with the Beavers

Lucy thought the Beavers had a very snug little home though it was not at all like Mr Tumnus's cave. There were no books or pictures, and instead of beds there were bunks, like on board ship, built into the wall. And there were hams and strings of onions hanging from the roof, and against the walls were gum boots and oilskins and hatchets and pairs of *shears* and spades and *trowels* and things for carrying *mortar* in and fishing-rods and fishing-nets and sacks. And the cloth on the table, though very clean, was very rough.

Just as the frying-pan was nicely hissing, Peter and Mr Beaver came in with the fish which Mr Beaver had already opened with his knife and cleaned out in the open air. You can think how good the new-caught fish smelled while they were frying and how the hungry children *longed* for them to be done and how very much hungrier still they had become before Mr Beaver said, "Now we're nearly ready." In a few minutes everyone was drawing up their stools (it was all three-legged stools in the Beavers' house except for Mrs Beaver's own special rocking-chair beside the fire) and preparing to enjoy themselves. There was a jug of creamy milk for the children (Mr Beaver stuck to beer) and a great big lump of deep yellow butter in the middle of the table from which everyone took as much as he wanted to go with his potatoes, and all the children thought – and I agree with them – that there's nothing to beat good freshwater fish if you eat it when it has been alive half an hour ago and has come out of the pan half a minute ago. And when they had finished the fish Mrs Beaver brought unexpectedly out of the oven a great and gloriously sticky marmalade roll, steaming hot, and at the same time moved the kettle on to the fire, so that when they had finished the marmalade roll the tea was made and ready to be poured out. And when each person had got his (or her) cup of tea, each person shoved back his (or her) stool so as to be able to lean against the wall and gave a long sigh of contentment.

"And now," said Mr Beaver, pushing away his empty beer mug and pulling his cup of tea towards him, "if you'll just wait till I've got my pipe lit up and going nicely – why, now we can get to business. It's snowing again," he added, *cocking* his eye at the window. "That's all the better, because it means we shan't have any visitors; and if anyone should have been trying to follow you, why he won't find any tracks."

*C.S. Lewis*

**Look up the words in italics in the dictionary section at the back.**

Write down their meaning.

 **Answer the questions.**

1. Describe the Beavers' home. Give a general impression, without mentioning all the details.
2. What do you think Mr Beaver had been doing outside before dinner?
3. What does Mr Beaver like to drink? Where does Mrs Beaver like to relax?
4. Explain what freshwater fish is. What other food was available?
5. Why did everybody give 'a long sigh of contentment'?

 **Find the words in the passage that have the same or similar meaning to the following.**

1. a deep breath
2. footprints
3. satisfaction
4. cloth waterproofed with oil

5. cosy
6. dealings; affairs
7. a shallow cooking vessel
8. pushed

 **Think about Lucy's character.**

1. What does she seem to be like? Think about the information she gives us and how her mind works. How alert is she to her surroundings?
2. How does the length of the sentences and punctuation convey how Lucy speaks to us?

 **Read the passage again.**

1. How is the final paragraph different from the rest of the passage? Think of at least two ways.
2. What do you think has happened just before this passage to Lucy and Peter? How can you tell?

# Litter Dump

1. Where do you think this photograph was taken?

2. What feelings does this scene arouse in you? Explain why.

3. Why do you think the photographer took this picture? What might the photographer be trying to say to you with such a picture? Is it well-taken?

4. List some of the objects you see in the picture. What in your opinion is the most unusual object? Give the reason for your choice.

5. How did all this rubbish end up here, in your opinion? Would it be correct to describe this form of pollution as 'toxic'? If all the rubbish were removed what would the scene be like?

6. Look at the lifebuoy. Think up an unusual story to explain how it came to be here.

7. Look at the ball. Was it lost or discarded? Who might once have owned it? If the ball were to tell its own story, what would it say?

8. If this photograph were to be used as an anti-pollution poster, what slogan would you create for it? If, on the other hand, a manufacturer of lifebuoys wanted to use it in an advertising campaign, can you think of any slogan or caption that would be appropriate?

# Bird's-eye View

1. Where do you think this girl is standing? What words would you use to describe the view she has?
2. What time of year is it? What kind of day? Is it very windy? How do you know? Describe the sky.
3. Give a description of the girl, paying particular attention to her hair.
4. What does she see immediately below her? Give some details.
5. What is the most interesting building in the middle distance? Describe it.
6. What can she see on the horizon?
7. Try to give some general statements about this town/city e.g. what is its size?
8. Give an estimate of how high the girl's position is above ground level. Have you ever had such a bird's-eye view? Where? Tell us about it.
9. How do you think the girl feels as she stands here – happy, nervous, sad, excited, adventurous or mischievous? (Give a reason for your choice.)
10. Think of a name for this girl. She turns around – what does she look like? Her best friend is with her – tell us about her or him. Why have they come to this spot? Conjure up a story about them.
11. What else comes to your mind as you look at this photograph?

# Should or Would?

Read the following.

*I will go to the see the film with you.* This tells us that I will definitely go.

*I **would** go to see the film with you **if** I had the money.* This tells us that going to see the film is dependent or conditional on having the money.

Words such as **would, could, should, if, may, might** are used in this way.

 **Write questions for these answers.**

    **1.** Sabina would have made the dress if you'd asked her.

    **2.** If Minnie had made the situation clear I would have gone with her.

    **3.** I would have supported the team last Saturday if Ricky had.

 **Write answers to these questions using** would, could, if **and** because.

    **1.** Could you complete the painting by next week?

    **2.** Would you expect Larry to make all the arrangements?

    **3.** Could you make it clear to Simon that he needs to hurry?

    **4.** Would he be able to collect the car in the morning?

 **Complete and write out these sentences using** if **or** then.

    **1.** I should always remember …

    **2.** I may learn how to …

    **3.** Karl might ring Mark …

    **4.** If I clear out that cupboard …

 **Complete these sentences using** should, may, might **and** if.

    **1.** … if I travel by train.

    **2.** … then I could plant the seeds.

    **3.** … if I could spare the time.

    **4.** … if the sea is warm.

# The Stadium

1. Without looking for any particular detail or name, can you in general terms describe the scene pictured here?

2. Examining the photograph more closely, try to guess in one sentence exactly what the occasion is.

3. Do you think the photograph is well taken? Why? Where is the vantage point of the photographer?

4. Can you find words to describe the stadium and the general throng of spectators?

5. What is taking place down on the playing pitch? What is the most striking feature there in your opinion? What do you think will happen next in this display?

6. Describe the people in the foreground. What do you think they are saying to one another?

7. What feelings does this photograph arouse in you – excitement, nervousness, joy? If you were there, where would you want to sit? What clothes would you wear? What would you take with you?

8. Try to imagine that you are one of the players in the dressing-room. What are you doing right now? What are the other players doing? How do you feel? What sounds do you hear outside the dressing room?

9. Think of your senses: sight, hearing, smell, touch, and even the fifth one, taste. Tell what happens next as you walk down the tunnel to the pitch.

# Story Endings

- Most stories involve a conflict or problem, to be resolved in one way or another. The conflict is resolved in the climax. For example, Jack kills the Giant (in the climax of *Jack and the Beanstalk*), or the Wolf is killed (in *Little Red Riding Hood*). We then come to the end of the story, or what in the movies is called the 'wrap up'. As a general rule, endings should not be lingered over – one or two paragraphs is probably long enough. Good endings can be achieved by describing the scene after the climax, or by telling what the main character has gained, lost or learned from the whole experience, or by tying up some loose ends. How you end your story is entirely up to you. Let your imagination do the work.

 **Think about it.**

1. Think of one of the books you have most enjoyed reading. How did the story end?
2. Jack has chopped down the beanstalk. The Giant is dead ... Write an ending to the story in the form of dialogue between Jack and his mother.

 **Draw the picture of the 'end scene' to the picture below and write the story ending. Give the story an interesting title.**

 **'My Terrible Invention'.**

The robot you invented has just caused havoc in your school. Write a suitable ending paragraph.

# Conjunctions

- A conjunction is a word which is used to join words, phrases and sentences together.
- Some common conjunctions:

| and | after | if | because | unless |
| but | while | as | since | for |
| either (or) | when | before | although | until |
| neither (nor) | both | yet | though | |

**Write out these sentences. Choose conjunctions from the above list to complete them.**

1. I tried to sing _____ my throat was too sore.
2. Neither Pauline _____ Dan turned up for rehearsals.
3. _____ you come or you stay, it's as simple as that.
4. I tried the cake _____ I thought it was delicious.
5. The game was cancelled _____ of the snow.
6. You should have checked your change _____ leaving the shop.
7. We will shelter here _____ the rain stops.
8. She continued to climb _____ her ankle was swelling fast.
9. "You will be fined _____ you move that car right now."
10. I was outside in the rain _____ he was inside in the warmth.

**Complete the following sentences, all of which begin with conjunctions.**

1. Although the tickets were expensive,
2. As soon as I saw the lions,
3. When I opened the parcel,
4. Since we have to get up early,
5. Unless you pay a deposit,
6. Because the star of the show is ill,
7. If you practise every day,

63

# The Diver

I put on my aqua-lung and plunge
Exploring, like a ship with a glass keel,
The secrets of the deep. Along my lazy road
On and on I steal —
Over waving bushes which at a touch explode
Into shrimps, then closing, rock to the tune of the tide;
Over crabs that vanish in puffs of sand,
Look, a string of pearls bubbling at my side
Breaks in my hand —
Those pearls were my breath!... Does that hollow hide
Some old Armada wreck in seaweed furled,
Crusted with barnacles, her cannon rusted,
The great San Phillip? What bullion in her hold?
Pieces of eight, silver crowns, and bars of solid gold?

I shall never know. Too soon the clasping cold
Fastens on flesh and limb
And pulls me to the surface. Shivering, back I swim
To the beach, the noisy crowds, the ordinary world.

*Ian Serraillier*

**Answer these questions.**

**1.** Find a line which describes a diver in motion and write it down.

**2.** 'Look, a string of pearls bubbling at my side

Breaks in my hand –

Those pearls were my breath!'

Write down how the writer could describe: a blue whale, a shark.

**3.** In some lines of the poem there are examples of assonance; where the middle vowels rhyme. For example, crab/vanish/sand in line 7. Find another example.

**4.** The Armada was a fleet of warships that set sail in 1588. Besides a cannon what other things does the diver imagine he could find in a wreck?

**5.** Why do you think the poem is divided into two parts?

**6.** What effect did the last four lines have on you? What feeling does it give you? (This is called connotation.) Do you think the diver is glad to be back in the ordinary world?

 **The rhyming pattern in the poem is quite complicated but you can find several examples if you look carefully.**

**1.** Find:

three pairs of end rhymes (for example, keel/steal),

two examples where three words all have the same end rhyme,

the word that rhymes with 'furled',

two words that rhyme at the beginning and end of a line.

**2.** There are many lines which 'run on' in the poem. This means you carry on reading after the line has finished. There are others which stop in the middle of a line:

'I shall never know. Too soon the clasping cold

Fastens on flesh and limb'

Find other examples of this in the poem.

**3.** Read the poem again, with expression, noting where you should stop and where you should read on. Decide where you feel the poem has an obvious rhyme and write down the words.

**4.** Say which lines seem to you to have a less obvious rhyme. Try to explain why you think this is.

# Sitting Bull, Last Great Indian Chief

At last on 19 July, 1881, Sitting Bull and 186 of his remaining followers crossed the border and rode into the nearest military fort. The Hunkpapa chief was wearing a calico shirt, a pair of shabby leggings and a dirty blanket. He looked old and beaten when he surrendered his rifle to the commanding officer.

Sitting Bull was held as a military prisoner for almost two years before he was transferred to the Hunkpapa *Reservation* at Standing Rock. But during this time Sioux chiefs and sub-chiefs from everywhere on the Great Reservation came to honour him. *Journalists* wanted interviews. Sitting Bull thought he had been forgotten. Instead he was famous.

In the summer of 1883 when the Northern Pacific Railroad drove the last spike in its track across the continent Sitting Bull was chosen to speak at the celebration. No other Indian was even considered.

Sitting Bull was to talk in the Sioux language; an interpreter was to translate his words into English. The big event occurred on September 8th in Bismarck. Sitting Bull was taken to the speakers' platform and introduced. "I hate all the white people," he began. "You are thieves and liars. You have taken away our land and made us outcasts." Knowing that only the interpreter could understand what he was saying, Sitting Bull paused for applause; he bowed, smiled and then continued his insults. At last he sat down and the *bewildered* interpreter took his place. By inventing a few friendly sentences and adding some well-worn Indian sayings he brought the audience to its feet with a standing *ovation* for Sitting Bull.

The following year William F. (Buffalo Bill) Cody decided to put the famous Chief in his Wild West Show. Crowds flocked to see Sitting Bull. Some booed the "Killer of Custer," but after each show these same people offered him money for copies of his signed photograph. Sitting Bull gave most of it away to the band of ragged, hungry boys who seemed to follow him everywhere.

After the tour ended he returned to Standing Rock with two farewell presents from Buffalo Bill – a big white *sombrero* and a performing horse.

Two years later Buffalo Bill invited Sitting Bull to go with the show on a tour of Europe, but the Chief refused. "I am needed here," he said. "There is more talk of the white man taking our lands."

*Dee Brown*

**Look up the words in italics in the dictionary section at the back.**

Write down their meaning.

 **Answer these questions.**

**1.** Who was Sitting Bull?
**2.** Why did Sitting Bull and his followers cross the border?
**3.** How do you know that Sitting Bull's fame spread far and wide?
**4.** Why was he so angry with the 'white man'?
**5.** How did the interpreter manage to avoid an uproar at the celebration?
**6.** Many white people had 'mixed feelings' about Sitting Bull. Why?
**7.** Who was Buffalo Bill? What did he do for a living?
**8.** Why did Sitting Bull not go to Europe with the show?
**9.** How do you think Sitting Bull's life changed from his days on the plains? What do you think he felt about this? (Think carefully.)

 **In what way is the passage a biography of Sitting Bull?**

Write down your answer.

 **Now explain what an autobiography is.**

Write the fourth paragraph again as an autobiography. Remember to use the first person, 'I'.

 **Imagine you are a journalist who has come to interview Sitting Bull at Standing Rock.**

- First decide what is the most important information you wish to find out about him.
- Next draw up a list of ten questions that you would ask him. Some questions may have specific answers. These are called 'closed questions'. (e.g. When did you finally cross the border?) You would probably ask these questions at the beginning of the interview.
- Other questions should be 'open questions' which have no specific answers (e.g. How did you feel about ... ?)
- Work with a partner. You should be the journalist, your partner should be Sitting Bull. Ask your questions and see how the interview works. Change any questions which do not seem to give you the information you want.

 **Write an article of 300 words based on your interview with Sitting Bull.**

Begin your article by describing your first impressions of Sitting Bull. Then select the most important information to include.

# Homophones

- Homophones are words which sound the same but are spelled differently.
  e.g. blue/blew   air/heir

 **Choose the correct word from each pair to fill in the blank spaces.**

1. Jim tackled the *(bare/bear)* with his *(bare/bear)* hands.
2. I will *(meat/meet)* you at the shops at five o'clock.
3. The ball smashed through the *(pane/pain)* of glass.
4. The wine is stored in the *(seller/cellar)*.
5. There will be a *(sail/sale)* in that shop next *(weak/week)*.
6. Paula *(knew/new)* the answers to all the questions.
7. Those flowers were *(grown/groan)* in his garden.
8. I had chocolate ice cream for *(desert/dessert)*.
9. We were shocked by his bad manners and *(course/coarse)* language.
10. If we work hard, the teacher will let us off *(hour/our)* homework.

 **Write one homophone for each of the following.**

| | | | |
|---|---|---|---|
| **1.** fair | **5.** male | **9.** beech | **13.** two |
| **2.** feet | **6.** board | **10.** heard | **14.** flour |
| **3.** made | **7.** isle | **11.** key | **15.** dew |
| **4.** hole | **8.** rain | **12.** threw | **16.** tire |

 **Try to find two homophones for each of these words.**

| | |
|---|---|
| **1.** raze | **4.** pair |
| **2.** you | **5.** sent |
| **3.** he'll | **6.** prays |

 **Write the homophones to match each pair of definitions.**

1. material spread over a surface          the place where a wild animal lies
2. a part of a plant                       white powder for making bread etc.
3. peep                                     a raised walkway over water

 # Write a Poem

- Everyone can write poetry and enjoy doing it! Here are two simple examples:

**1.** Let's say we want to write a poem about 'winter'. First, make a note of the things that come to mind when you relax and think of 'winter' – snow, robin redbreast, storms, the 'flu ... and so on. From your list pick, say, seven things that you would really like to include in your poem. Take each one in turn and write a single line for it. Take 'snow' for example:

One line could be:

    Winter is ...   the soft swishing snow

    or

    Winter is ...   the swish of snow on my windowpane

    or

    Winter is ...   the breath of snow on the frosted pane

As soon as you are happy with Line 1 move on to Line 2. You could make them rhyme if you like:

    Winter is ...   the breath of snow on the frosted pane

                the hungry robin at the door again

Or without rhyme, if you prefer:

    Winter is ...   the breath of snow on the frosted pane

    Winter is ...   a silent robin on a solitary bare tree

Now try your hand at it ... write a poem on any subject you like ...
Mondays, Summer, happiness or monsters? Illustrate your poem with a picture.

**2.** Next we will write an acrostic poem. This is where we write the subject of the poem vertically, to give us the first letter of each line. Here's a poem, 'DOGS':

    Digging up gardens for bones

    Or chasing cats or

    Growling at Postmen

    Sniff, sniff, sniff ...

Try some of your own acrostic poems. Here are some suggestions.
cats, eels, toys, rain, snow, bikes, games, sweets, ghosts, movies.

# Catastrophe

In February we celebrated Tootsie's first birthday. She carried on a family *tradition* of smashing her fist into her birthday cake. Grandma, who believes in handing out gifts for everyone, not just the birthday person, brought me a four-colour ballpoint pen, and Fudge a new Brian Tumkin book.

"Read!" Fudge told Grandma.

She took him on her lap and read him the latest story about Uriah, Brian Tumkin's favourite character.

"I used to really like his books when I was a little kid," I said.

"I'm not a little kid," Fudge reminded me. "Next year I'll be in first grade. You want to see a little kid, look at the birthday girl!"

The birthday girl was sitting in her high-chair making a mess. Grandma had brought her a new baby-proof cup, one that refused to turn over no matter how hard Tootsie tried. Finally, Tootsie screeched, picked up the cup and dumped her milk over her head.

"Tootsie's first birthday party could go down as a real *catastrophe*," I said.

"What's a castradophie?" Fudge asked.

"It's when something goes wrong," I said.

"It's when everything goes wrong," Mom added.

Talk about catastrophes! Six weeks later Tootsie learned to walk. At first it was just a few feet at a time, from Mom to Dad, or from me to Fudge. But pretty soon she was toddling all over the place. Sometimes she'd crash-land and if no one was watching, she'd laugh and start over again. But if she caught one of us looking at her, she'd start bawling and wouldn't stop until she got an arrowroot cookie.

And Tootsie wasn't the only one crash-landing. Fudge was learning to ride his bicycle. One of his major problems was stopping. Instead of using his brakes, he kept trying to jump off while his bike was still going. I was wrong when I told him he might get a couple of scraped knees. Elbows, knees, head was more like it. *Constantly*. But he refused to give up. He was really determined to get to ride to school.

Finally, towards the end of April, Mom and Dad decided that Fudge had mastered the art of bike-riding well enough to ride to school ... And it would have turned out okay, if only Fudge had remembered to use his brakes when he got to the bike rack at school. But he didn't. So he crashed into the rack, knocking down a pile of bikes, and he wound up with scraped elbows, scraped knees, and torn jeans.

*Judy Blume*

 **Look up the words in italics in the dictionary section at the back.**

Write down their meaning.

 **Answer the questions.**

**1.** What gifts did Grandma bring with her?
**2.** What is a 'baby-proof' cup?
**3.** Why might the party turn out to be a 'catastrophe'?
**4.** Exactly how old was Tootsie when she learned to walk?
**5.** Why was it better to pretend not to notice if the baby fell?
**6.** What difficulty did Fudge have with his bike?
**7.** What happened on the first day Fudge road his bike to school?
**8.** Which words tell you that this is by an American writer? Write the words that we would use instead.

 **Author style.**

We all write in different ways according to what we are writing about and who we are writing for. For example, if we were applying for a job we would be writing in a formal style. If we were writing a story about a wizard, we would be writing a fantasy. However, most authors have their own personal style. We can often recognise it in the different books they write.

You are going to contrast  (compare the difference) between two authors:
**1.** Make two columns in your book with the headings:

*Catastrophe (Judy Blume)*          *The Rider (J.R.R. Tolkien)*

**2.** Read 'Catastrophe' again and read 'The Rider' on page 92.
**3.** Select the words from those below that fit each passage and write them under the correct column. You should not classify all words but each column should have at least seven words in it. You may use the same words in both columns, but be careful, they need to be suitable. Then add words of your own.

> adventurous  plenty of characters   not much dialogue   a thriller
> fantasy   difficult to read   easy to visualise   a family story   everyday
> highly descriptive language   humorous   cartoon   realistic   strange
> reassuring   easy to read   about good and evil   western   formal

**4.** Now write an account of both passages, saying what the authors' styles are like. Write two paragraphs. The first paragraph should deal with one passage, the second with the other. Use the information in your columns to show the difference between the passages.

Use terms such as: However ... , By contrast ... , As well as ... .

# Prefixes

- A prefix is placed at the beginning of a word or part of a word to change its meaning in some way.

  For example, the prefix trans- means 'across'... e.g. transatlantic, transfer.

**A** Place the prefix TRANS- before the following.
Write down what you think each new word means.

**1.** P O R T     **2.** L A T E     **3.** P L A N T
**4.** F O R M     **5.** F I X

**B** The prefix SUB- means 'under'. Write one word (containing sub- as a prefix) to match each of the following definitions.

**1.** an undersea vessel used in warfare     S U B
**2.** the outlying areas of a town or city     S U B
**3.** one who takes the place of another     S U B
**4.** words printed on a television or film screen     S U B
**5.** to sink in water     S U B
**6.** underground passage or tunnel     S U B

**C** The prefix PRE- means 'in front of'. Write each matching word.

**1.** care taken beforehand     P R E
**2.** to tell of something before it happens     P R E
**3.** to save from injury or loss or decay     P R E
**4.** to take for granted     P R E
**5.** a doctor's note advising medicine     P R E
**6.** make ready     P R E

**D** Try to give three more examples of each of these prefixes.

| RE- | AB- | EX- |
|---|---|---|
| repair | absorb | explain |

# Antonyms

● Antonyms are words that are opposite in meaning. e.g. high/low   big/small

 **A** **Write the antonym for each word.**

ENTRANCE

rude          guilty
hero          fresh
freedom       personal
barren        narrow
advance       destruction
deep          minimum
superior      entrance
feminine      stupid
ancient       temporary

 **B** **Add a prefix to give the antonym for each word.**

flexible      responsible
imaginative   pure
legal         regular
please        moral
necessary     orderly
like          normal
common        obey

 **C** **Change the prefix to give the antonym for each word.**

export        descend       leftward
explode       internal      increase

 **D** **Rewrite these sentences giving the opposite of the words in italics.**

**1.** Helen *purchased* a *new* bike last *winter*.
**2.** Jim's *positive* attitude was *praised* in the report.
**3.** We moved *slowly* across the *barren highlands*.
**4.** The captain believed that *victory* was *possible*.

# Choosing the Right Word

● Taking time and making an effort to choose the right word – whether noun, adjective, verb or adverb – will make all the difference to your writing. (A dictionary and thesaurus will assist greatly.)

**A** **Suggest a suitable adjective, verb and adverb for each of the following. Then combine them in either one or two interesting sentences. (The first one is done for you.)**

|  | ADJECTIVE | VERB | ADVERB |
|---|---|---|---|

**1.** Blackbeard the Pirate's voice:　　1. gruff　　　2. snarled　　3. menacingly

*I shuddered when I heard Blackbeard's gruff voice. "Walk the plank!" he snarled menacingly.*

**2.** Wind on a stormy night.

**3.** Sunshine on water.

**4.** A mouse eating.

**5.** A jet taking off.

**6.** A clown performing.

**7.** A lifeguard carrying out a rescue.

**8.** A cyclist escaping injury.

# Similes

- You will describe characters or their actions more clearly if you use similes. A simile compares two things which are alike.
- Similes usually begin with the words 'like' or 'as'.
  *Example:* I was like a statue and as white as a sheet.

**A** **Make similes using the adjectives below.**

quick  hot  old  strong  hungry  busy  black  slow  heavy  light  blind  fit

**B** **Think of certain action words and write complete sentences using the following similes.**

*Example:* I fled like a bat out of hell when my ball smashed the window.

1. like a bull in a china shop
2. like a hawk
3. like a knife cutting through butter
4. like a fish out of water

5. like a grasshopper
6. like a bird without feathers
7. like a hot potato
8. like a hero

**C** **Complete the similes.**

proud       as a swan
slippery     as a peacock
cunning     as an eel
graceful     as a fox

**D** **Look at the picture and describe what happened next. Use your own similes.**

75

# Little Water Wanderer

The eldest and biggest of the litter was a dog-cub, and when he drew his first breath he was less than five inches long from his nose to where his wee tail joined his back. His fur was soft and grey as the buds of the willow before they open at Eastertide. He was called Tarka, which was the name given to otters many years ago by men dwelling in hut circles on the moor. It means Little Water Wanderer, or, Wandering as Water.

With his two sisters he *mewed* when hungry, seeking the warmth of his mother, who uncurled and held up a paw whenever tiny pads would stray in her fur, and tiny noses snuffle against her. She was careful that they should be clean, and many times in the nights and days of their blind helplessness she rolled on her back, ceasing her kind of purr to twist her head and lick them. And sometimes her short ears would stiffen as she started up, her eyes fierce with a *tawny* glow and the coarse hair of her neck *bristling*, having heard some dangerous sound. By day the dog was far away, sleeping in a holt by the weir-pools which had its rocky entrance underwater, but in the darkness his whistle would move the fierceness from her eyes, and she would lie down to sigh happily as her young struggled to draw life from her.

This was her first litter, and she was overjoyed when Tarka's lids ungummed, and his eyes peeped upon her, blue and wondering. He was then eleven days old. Before the coming of her cubs, her world had been a wilderness, but now her world was in the eyes of her firstborn. After a day of sight-seeing he began to play, tapping her nose with a paw and biting her whiskers. He kicked against the other cubs, and his eyes darkened, and he tried harder than ever to bite his mother's whiskers, which tickled him when he was being held between her paws and washed. Once, when he was milk-happy and had snarled his first snarl without frightening her into stopping the licking of his belly, he was so furious that he tried to bite off her head. She opened her mouth and panted, which is the way otters laugh among themselves, while he kicked and struggled, and she pretended to bite through his neck. Tarka was not afraid, and clawed her whiskers and struggled to be free. His mother released him very gently; on wobbly legs he returned to the *assault* of her head, but he *snarled* so much that he was sick; and when she had tidied him he fell asleep under her throat.

When his eyes had been opened a fortnight, Tarka knew so much that he could crawl as far as a yard from her, and stay away although in her anxiety she mewed to him to return. She was afraid of the daylight by the opening of the holt, but Tarka had no fear.

*Henry Williamson*

 **Look up the words in italics in the dictionary section at the back.**

Write down their meaning.

 **Answer the questions.**

**1.** Describe Tarka when he was first born.

**2.** What happened when he was eleven days old?

**3.** How does an otter react to danger?

**4.** In what ways did the mother show she cared for her young?

**5.** Where do you think Tarka's father was?

**6.** What game did Tarka play with his mother?

**7.** Why did he snarl at her?

**8.** Why did his mother not let him wander away from her?

 **Read the following.**

> **Tarka The Otter** *by Henry Williamson*
>
> *'This was her first litter, and she was overjoyed when Tarka's lids ungummed, and his eyes peeped upon her, blue and wondering.'*
>
> Thirty nine miles from Cranmere Tarn to the Morte Stone 'as the falcon glides' is a hard journey for a young otter and Tarka learns much in the process.
>
> With great technical skill and dedication to the truth, Henry Williamson takes us through the Devon countryside on a journey we are unlikely to forget.

The account above is called a 'blurb'. It is usually found on the back cover of a book or novel and is a comment or synopsis of the story. While it tells the would-be reader what the book is about, it also advertises it.

**1.** Decide which parts of the blurb are quotations from the book. How can you tell?

**2.** Write down which part you think tries to advertise the book. Explain why.

 **Write your own blurbs.**

**1.** Write a blurb of not more than 75 words for a passage of your own choice from this text book. Remember to choose a suitable quotation.

**2.** Now write a blurb for the last book you read, or the one you are reading now.

# Interjections

- Interjections are exclamations, where words are cried out in anger, surprise, sorrow, joy, relief, etc.

  Examples: "Ouch!" shouted the girl when the hammer fell on her toe.

  "What a terrible thing to happen!" gasped Mrs Baker on hearing of the accident.

- An exclamation mark (!) is usually written after an interjection.

 **Write a suitable sentence for each of the following interjections. Insert quotation marks where necessary.**

| | | | |
|---|---|---|---|
| **1.** Hurrah! | | **5.** Time up! |
| **2.** Halt! | | **6.** Oh! |
| **3.** Hush! | | **7.** Ha! Ha! |
| **4.** Help! | | **8.** Whew! |

 **Write the exclamations that each of these people might make.**

**1.** A person admiring Niagara Falls.

**2.** Howard Carter on discovering the tomb of Tutankhamun in Egypt.

**3.** Batman on hearing of the latest robbery by The Joker.

**4.** Arnold Schwarzenegger on being asked to star as Tarzan in his next movie.

**5.** An astronaut on setting foot on Venus.

**6.** Someone who has just won a million pounds.

 **Write a paragraph about this picture. Include at least three interjections/exclamations somewhere in the paragraph.**

# Inventions

The more you know about words, the more you can play with them.
For example you can combine prefixes and suffixes to make new words.

**mega** *means large*          **vacca** *means cow*

So, **megavacca** could mean a large cow!

 **A**  **Match these prefixes and suffixes to their correct meanings by writing them out.**

| Prefixes | | Suffixes | |
|---|---|---|---|
| anti | small | ative | name |
| auto | above | craft | little |
| hemi | sound | itis | fear |
| hyper | self | ish | without |
| kilo | against | less | inflame |
| micro | too much | nym | full of |
| phone | thousand | ous | skill |
| super | half | phobia | power |

 **B**  **When you have checked that A is correct, make as many new words as you can.**

You can use a prefix or suffix more than once.

# Reviewing a Book

 All books fall into two main categories, non-fiction or fiction. Non-fiction refers to books that are based on facts in the real world. A book of fiction springs from the author's imagination. Such stories fall into different classes or categories – adventure, fantasy, mystery, science fiction, historical fiction, animal story, etc. In reviewing fiction, try to sum up the plot in a clear, brief way, and give some details on the main character(s). In giving your reaction to the book it is very important to be able to support your criticism, whether positive or negative. If you find a book 'interesting' or 'exciting' or 'dull', make sure that you are able to give your reasons why. Think up your own system for rating the book, e.g. ***** for excellent to * for boring. (Show your rating system at the bottom of the page.)

**A** **Write a review of a book you have recently read, using these headings.**

Book review

Title

Author

Category

The plot

Main character(s)

The climax

The ending

Reaction

Rating

# Haiku Calendar

Haiku is a form of Japanese poetry. The traditional haiku is written in three lines of seventeen syllables: 5 – 7 – 5. The poem is like an ordinary picture, seen from a special viewpoint and the seasons or time of day are often mentioned.

When you write a haiku poem try not to use lots of adjectives. Everyday language can be used. You should write in the present tense as if it is happening now and you should try not to use 'I'. This is to help the reader share the poem more easily.

 **Read the following haiku and decide why the series is called Haiku Calendar.**

Count the number of syllables in the lines.

the spring air tranquil
two petals of peach blossom
settle on the yard

midsummer heat wave
turning the city street white
our eyes are shining

impatient evening
the wind is chasing the moon
across autumn skies

one winter heron
picks its way among shallows
a tail feather drifts

*Mary Green*

 **Write your own haiku on your own or with a friend.**

Choose a season or a particular time of day or, if you have seen something unusual, write about that. Try to write using the traditional form: 5 – 7 – 5 and follow the advice above.

# Isolation

1. What name is given to this type of dwelling? Try, in one sentence, to give the name, location and condition of this building.

2. Think of as many words as you can to describe the poor condition of this building, e.g. derelict, dilapidated, etc.

3. Looking at the dwelling in more detail, describe the particular features you notice.

4. Besides the poor condition of the building, what other evidence is there to suggest that no one lives there?

5. What signs are there that some care is still being taken of the cottage? If you opened the door and walked inside, what do you think you would find?

6. In what ways does this place differ from your home? Try to think of as many comparisons as possible.

7. When, roughly, do you think this cottage was built? How do you think it was built? Describe how you imagine it looked back then (outside, inside, the surroundings).

8. Who do you think may have lived there? What kind of life do you think its owner(s), or perhaps tenants, lived? Would you have liked to have lived in those days?

9. Think for a few moments, if you were to write a story set in this location, what would it be? What title or name would you give to your story?

# Dialogue

● The conversation between the characters in your story is called dialogue. As well as telling us more about the characters, dialogue is very important in moving the plot or storyline forward.

 **Look back to the stories 'The Circus' and 'Dad the Poacher'.**

Roughly, what percentage of each was dialogue?

 **Write the dialogue that you think might have taken place between the people in this picture.**

 **Write the dialogue.**

Your dog has attacked Cuddles, a prize-winning Persian cat belonging to your neighbour, Mr Bully. He knocks on your door in a very angry mood.

 **Write the dialogue that might occur between a doctor and his/her patients on an unusual hospital ward.**

The patients can be suffering from various injuries or ailments – fear of doctors; missing brain; enlarged eyebrow – anything you like!

# At the Beach

**1.** In which country do you think this photograph was taken? What do the group of people in this photo have in common?

**2.** How would you describe the mood of the people here? Why are many of the people smiling? What do you think they are all doing here?

**3.** Give an accurate description that would clearly identify one individual in the photograph.

**4.** Which person in the photograph interests you most? Why? Try to give some imaginary details about this person.

**5.** Look at the white objects just by the edge of the sea. What are they? Have you ever been in one? How does it work?

**6.** Look at the umbrellas. What different materials are they made from? Can you describe them to a friend?

**7.** Suggest a title for the photograph.

**8.** Have you been on holiday recently? Where did you go? Did you like it? Why?

**9.** Choose two people from the photograph. Dramatise a conversation between them. Either improvise or prepare the dialogue beforehand.

# Writing For Different Purposes

We can write in different ways depending on who we are writing to. A letter to a friend is different from a letter to a bank manager. When we write to a friend we write casually or informally, as if we were chatting to them. When we write to a bank manager we use a more formal or business-like tone.

 **Copy this table into your book and tick the correct box for each example.**

| A letter: | Formal | Informal |
|-----------|--------|----------|
| to your sister  who is on holiday | | |
| cancelling a dentist appointment | | |
| thanking the Queen for tea | | |
| to your friend who is ill | | |
| to the tax inspector | | |
| to a pop star from a fan | | |

 **Look at these examples.**

When we write in a formal tone the voice will sound more distant or impersonal, particularly if we are complaining. We could use the passive like this:

Mr Swindler
The Bank Manager
Grabitall Bank
10 February 1999

Dear Mr Swindler

Thank you for your letter of 10th October. With regard to your comments concerning my request for a loan of £1000 ...

- If we were writing informally we might say: *When I asked you for a loan of £1000, you said that ...*

 **Write two letters of three paragraphs each.**

One should be to a cousin telling them about an expensive game you have bought which does not work. The other should be a letter of complaint to the shop where you bought it. Point out that you saved up for the game for a long time. Remember to write in an impersonal voice when you write formally.

# Creating a Different Impression

We can create different effects when we write. We can write in simple or complex sentences, short or long ones. We can shift words, clauses and phrases around, so that the writing sounds different when we read it.

 **Read the following.**

*The she-lion moved stealthily through the undergrowth. The young zebra was oblivious to her soft tread. She crouched and waited. Her eyes were alert. Her paws were set square in front. The zebra shifted nervously. He had at last caught the smell of lion. He scraped his hoof on the dry earth. He moved to the centre of the herd.*

**1.** How many sentences have been used?

We could write this account much more interestingly, so that tension is built up. If we combine sentences we will hear the voice change as we read.

*The she-lion moved stealthily through the undergrowth, the young zebra oblivious to her soft tread. She crouched and waited, her eyes alert, her paws set square in front. The zebra, at last catching the smell of lion, shifted nervously, scraped his hoof on the dry earth and moved to the centre of the herd.*

**2.** How many sentences have been used now?

 **Write the paragraph in another way, using long and short sentences.**

Which paragraph do you prefer? Try to write down why.

 **Now finish the description.**

You could begin by writing short sentences and turn them into longer ones later. You may wish to experiment, writing in different ways, until you achieve the effect you want. You will need to redraft your work.

# Writing Non-fiction

## (1) Researching the Story

- We have looked at the writing of fiction, that is, stories which spring from the writer's own imagination. Non-fiction, on the other hand, is concerned with stories which are based on facts in the real world. This writing may be in the form of a book, project or a newspaper article. The key to success is research and planning.

 **Read again 'Tigers on the brink' on page 16.**

List all the facts/figures that are given in the article.

**Give the basic facts/details (e.g. names of people, places, etc) of two recent news stories that you can recall.**

**You have been asked to write an article on your school for a local magazine.**

First of all, write down some of the basic facts you already know about your school. Secondly, list the questions which you would like to ask in order to gain further information about the school.

## (2) Planning the Story

- In writing fiction, we looked at the 'plot', which is the basic plan of the story. In writing non-fiction there is a need to have a plan of a similar nature. One simple way to do this is to map out the paragraph structure, noting down the main idea of each successive paragraph.

 **Complete the plan.**

An article consisting of eight paragraphs is to be written about foxes. The main idea of the first three paragraphs is given. Complete the rest of the story plan.

1. A glimpse of a particular fox.
2. Foxes in general.
3. Fox cubs.

# Whales

Whales are not fish. They belong to an order of mammals known as Cetaceans, a grouping which covers over 80 different species including dolphins and porpoises. Cetaceans evolved from animals that once lived on land. They are warm-blooded and they breathe air.

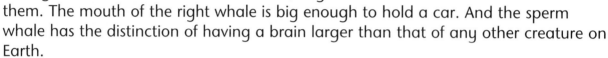

Whales are larger than all other animals. The arteries of the blue whale are so large that a small child could crawl through them. The mouth of the right whale is big enough to hold a car. And the sperm whale has the distinction of having a brain larger than that of any other creature on Earth.

Whales can be divided into two groups: Mysticeti and Odontoceti. Mysticeti means 'moustached whales'. Instead of teeth these whales have 'moustaches' of baleen (a substance similar in structure to the material out of which your fingernails are made). The baleen hangs from the roof of the mouth and acts like a *sieve* in taking large quantities of small food out of the water. The whale takes a great gulp of water, the food – called plankton – is filtered through the baleen, and then the water is expelled by the tongue. The grey whale of the Eastern Pacific is one such whale. It holds the record for the longest migration of any mammal. At the end of summer it will leave its feeding grounds in Alaska and swim all the way down the west coast of America until it reaches the *lagoons* of Baja California in Mexico. Here the whales will breed and calve before setting off on the return journey. The total distance involved is roughly 16,000km. Grey whales are very friendly and seem to like all the attention they get from whalewatchers. Many of them swim up to the whalewatchers' dinghies and lift their heads out of the water to be scratched.

It hardly needs to be said that the killer whale – or orca, as it is sometimes called – has no such reputation for friendliness. It belongs to the group known as Odontoceti, meaning 'whales with teeth'. Killer whale is a somewhat harsh name for this creature which only hunts to survive like any other carnivore. It feeds on a wide variety of prey such as fish, sea birds, seals, dolphins and sometimes other whales. It is a superbly equipped hunter. Its sense of hearing is finely developed. It can power through the water at speeds of 55km/h. And it has massive jaws, consisting of 26 sets of interlocking teeth. Quite a *formidable* enemy!

The global whale population is under threat today both from the whaling industry and from pollution. The situation has reached a point where the International Whaling Commission (I.W.C.) had to *intervene* and force a moratorium (temporary ban). Whales are still endangered, however, as some countries continue to hunt these remarkable creatures.

*Pierce Feirtear*

**Look up the words in italics in the dictionary section at the back.**

Write down their meaning.

 **Answer these questions.**

**1.** What do whales, dolphins and porpoises have in common?
**2.** What record does the sperm whale hold?
**3.** What does the term 'Odontoceti' mean?
**4.** Why are 'moustached whales' called this?
**5.** How does the 'moustached whale' obtain its food?
**6.** Where does the grey whale of the Eastern Pacific breed?
**7.** What makes the orca whale such an excellent hunter?

 **Skim through paragraph three. (Read through quickly – a good way, is to read down the middle section of the paragraph, if you can.)**

Write down one sentence which sums up the paragraph.

 **Read the passage again.**

**1.** Make notes of the main points in the other paragraphs.
**2.** Write one paragraph of your own, of 150 words, which summarises the passage.
**3.** Write a paragraph saying whether or not the passage gave you useful information about whales and what other types of information it could have included.

 **Find out about dolphins, porpoises or other sea creatures similar to whales.**

You will need to use ICT or research in the library. Write an account in the same style as the passage in 450 words. Use terms such as: It hardly needs to be said ..., In addition to ... .

**F** **Redraft your work, present it well and make it available as a resource for other children in the class to read.**

# Knowing the Right Word

**A** **Rewrite the sentences. Insert WERE, WHERE, WEAR, or WE'RE.**

● Remember: WERE is the plural form of was, WEAR means 'to be dressed in',
WE'RE means 'we are'. WHERE means 'in what place'.
**1.** _____ did you buy that hat?
**2.** The guards did not know _____ the prisoners _____ hiding.
**3.** "_____ on our way," said the pilot as the plane sped down the runway.
**4.** "I'm certain _____ going in the right direction," said the guide.
**5.** We made up our minds that we _____ not going to _____ costumes.
**6.** _____ _____ you when the tornado struck?
**7.** There _____ many people who _____ delayed because of the roadworks.
**8.** Our patience begins to _____ when _____ tired.

**B** **Rewrite the sentences. Insert AMONG or BETWEEN.**

● 'Among' is used when sharing something among more than two people.
'Between' is used when sharing something between two persons or things.
**1.** Anna and Tom shared the prize-money _____ them.
**2.** The teacher divided the sweets _____ the pupils.
**3.** I spotted my brother _____ the spectators.
**4.** There were many weeds _____ the flowers.
**5.** A white horse was standing _____ the two chestnut trees.

**C** **PRACTICE or PRACTISE?**

● 'Practice' is a noun, meaning: the exercise that is done to improve a skill.
'Practise' is a verb, meaning: to exercise to improve a skill.
**1.** You should always _____ what you preach.
**2.** Tennis _____ will take place on Saturday at 2 p.m.
**3.** I spent all afternoon at piano _____ .
**4.** I _____ the piano every evening.

**D** **Write a single word for each of the following.**

**a.** go up       **b.** go down      **c.** go forward
**d.** put off (an appointment)   **e.** put out (a fire)    **f.** put up with (a discomfort)

# Revision

 **List the nouns in the following sentences.**

'Whales belong to an order of mammals known as Cetaceans, a grouping which covers over 80 different species including dolphins and porpoises.'

 **List the adjectives.**

'Suddenly I noticed a dark shape gliding past in the crystal-clear waters beneath our flimsy boat. I could tell immediately that it was a shark. A cold shiver of fear ran down my spine … '

 **List the verbs.**

Uggy the Squirrel wanted those peanuts. He ran along the fence and hopped into the garden. He paused for a moment to make sure the coast was clear then scurried across the lawn. The sparrows chirped angrily as he dashed towards the bird table. "Here's that nutter again!" they roared. "Grab the food and fly!"

 **List the adverbs.**

The children cried excitedly when a dolphin suddenly leaped out of the water. "Give me the camera," said John urgently. "I've waited all day for this photograph." The dolphin, however, was too quick for him. It immediately dived, vanishing without trace.

 **Proof-read the following and divide it into three paragraphs.**

Everyone believed that the titanic was unsinkeable. Perhaps this was the reason why only enuff lifeboats for half off the passangers were placed on board. Tickets for her maiden voyaje were snapt up eagerly, and their were over 2,000 people on bored when it set out from southampton for new york on april 11 th 1912. Disaster was to strike after only four days at sea. the liner was ploughing threw calm seas at a speed of 22 nots. She had enterd an area known as Glass Banks when radio reports from other ships were recieved warning of icebergs. the warnings were ignored. The titantic steamed ahead at full speed it was almost midnight when frederick fleet, the look-out in the crow's nest, suddenly spotted an iceberg looming ahead in the darkness. he cried out a warning but it was too late to prevent a colision. a huge whole was ripped in to the side of the liner and the water pored in. At first the passengers treated the insident as a joke, yet, within minutes, the water had risen five metres inside the ship. Distress signels where sent out to the nearby liner, california, but her radio had unfortunately been switched of. Panic now spread as the huge liner listed to won side and began to sink.

# The Rider

They were beginning to look out for a place off the Road, where they could camp for the night, when they heard a sound that brought fear back into their hearts: the noise of hoofs behind them. They looked back, but they could not see far because of the many windings and rollings of the Road. As quickly as they could they scrambled off the beaten way and up into the deep heather and bilberry brushwood on the slopes above, until they came to a small patch of thick-growing hazels. As they peered out from among the bushes, they could see the Road, faint and grey in the failing light, some thirty feet below them. The sound of hoofs drew nearer. They were going fast, with a light clippety-clippety-clip. Then faintly, as if it was blown away from them by the breeze, they seemed to catch a *dim* ringing, as of small bells tinkling.

"That does not sound like a Black Rider's horse!" said Frodo, listening intently. The other hobbits agreed hopefully that it did not, but they all remained full of suspicion. They had been in fear of pursuit for so long that any sound from behind seemed *ominous* and unfriendly. But Strider was now leaning forward, stooped to the ground, with a hand to his ear, and a look of joy on his face.

The light faded, and the leaves on the bushes rustled softly. Clearer and nearer now the bells jingled, and clippety-clip came the quick trotting feet. Suddenly into view below came a white horse, gleaming in the shadows, running swiftly. In the dusk its *headstall* flickered and flashed, as if it were studded with gems like living stars. The rider's cloak streamed behind him, and his hood was thrown back; his golden hair flowed *shimmering* in the wind of his speed. To Frodo it appeared that a white light was shining through the form and *raiment* of the rider, as if through a thin veil.

Strider sprang from hiding and dashed down towards the Road, leaping with a cry through the heather; but even before he had moved or called, the rider had reined in his horse and halted, looking up towards the thicket where they stood. When he saw Strider he dismounted and ran to meet him calling out: "Ai na vedui Dunadan! Mae govannen!" His speech and clear ringing voice left no doubt in their hearts: the rider was of the Elven-folk.

*J.R.R. Tolkien*

**Look up the words in italics in the dictionary section at the back.**

Write down their meaning.

 **Answer these questions.**

1. Where did they intend to camp for the night?
2. What noise frightened them? Why?
3. Which sentence tells us that these hobbits have been fearful for some time?
4. When they listened carefully what other sound did they hear?
5. Why did Strider dash down towards the Road? How did he know?
6. What convinced the hobbits that they had nothing to fear from the rider?

 **Theme.**

A theme is an idea which interests an author and which runs through a story. It is like a hidden meaning. You need to think what the idea or message of a story might be. It may not come to you straight away.

1. Decide what themes (from the list) are involved in the passage.
   good and evil   horses   fear   other worlds   nature   camping   courage
2. Why have you chosen them? Comment using quotations from the passage.

 **Write an extended story.**

This is a story that should have several chapters and should be written over a period of time. Although you may change your ideas as you go, you will need to plan for your story and to put aside a time for writing it each week.

One way to begin is to think of a theme. Choose one theme from the passage above or one from a story you are familiar with. Then decide what type of story you will write. For example, for the theme of good and evil (a theme often found in tales of fantasy) you could weave a story about a powerful figure from another world, such as a mysterious figure who is threatening goodness.

You would then decide:
● who are to be the main characters  (the hero/heroine, someone who would defeat evil and the villain who would eventually be overcome)
● the setting or location of your story (such as a land between two worlds)
● the storyline (at this stage you would need only a rough outline).

You should add other characters and details later. Now plan your story! Whatever you choose, make sure your theme runs through the chapters. When you have finished your story ask yourself this question:
Can I find other themes in it which I did not know would be there?

## A.

**account** (n): a statement of money owed, spent, or received.

**ample** (adj): large enough; spacious.

**amplify** (v): to increase.

**artery** (n): a tube that carries blood around the body.

**artiste** (n): a professional entertainer.

**assault** (n): an attack.

**authority** (n): a person or group of people holding power.

## B.

**bewilder** (v): to confuse, lead astray.

**bewildered** (adj): confused.

**bewilderment** (n): confusion.

**bristle** (v): to stand up stiffly (esp. of hair).

**bulwark** (n): a means of defence.

## C.

**calorie** (n): a unit for measuring the energy in food.

**cataclysm** (n): a huge upheaval.

**cataclysmic** (adj): e.g. 'a cataclysmic flood'.

**catastrophe** (n): a sudden disaster.

**catastrophic** (adj): e.g. 'a catastrophic error'.

**cholesterol** (n): a fatty substance that can clog arteries.

**cock** (v): to set in an upright position.

**'cock the eye'**: glance knowingly.

**'cock one's nose'**: look disdainful.

**'cock-eyed'**: squinting.

**concertina** (n): a musical instrument similar to the accordion.

**constantly** (adv): always; often.

**covet** (v): to wish to possess that which belongs to another.

**covetous** (adj): extremely greedy.

## D.

**dim** (adj): not clear-sounding; not bright.

**douse** (v): drench with water.

**draught** (n): a pull. 'draught-animal': an animal used for pulling heavy loads.

## F.

**fable** (n): a story with a moral.

**fabulous** (adj): wonderful.

**formidable** (adj): fearsome.

## G.

**gaunt** (adj): thin.

**gleam** (v): to shine (faintly).

**glint** (n): a flash.

**glisten** (v): to gleam, i.e. to shine (faintly).

**grim** (adj): stern, harsh.

**grove** (n): a small wood.

## H.

**headstall** (n): the part of a bridle that fits around a horse's head.

**hind** (adj): placed at the back.

**hindsight** (n): wisdom after an event has happened.

**hind-leg** (n): back leg of an animal.

**holocaust** (n): a terrible destruction.

## I.

**indulgence** (n): free enjoyment.

**intervene** (v): to interfere, to step in and take action.

**intervention** (n): interference.

## J.

**journalism** (n): the profession of someone who writes for a newspaper.

**journalist** (n): someone who writes for a newspaper.

## L.

**lagoon** (n): a shallow saltwater lake (usually separated from the sea by a sandbank).

**literally** (adv): actually, in a real sense.

**long** (v): to wish.

**M.**

**materialise** (v): to appear in bodily form.

**mew** (v): cry like a cat.

**mortar** (n): a type of cement; a piece of artillery for launching bombs.

**N.**

**nutrition** (n): food.

**nutritional; nutritious** (adj): nourishing.

**O.**

**odour** (n): smell.

**ominous** (adj): of bad omen; inauspicious; unlucky.

**omen** (n): a sign of some event in the future that might bring good or evil.

**ovation** (n): loud applause.

**P.**

**pelt** (n): skin.

**plaint** (n): a sorrowful song.

**plaintive** (adj): sorrowful.

**plateau** (n): level land on high ground.

**plume** (n): a feather; anything of feathery appearance.

**plume** (v): to preen; to strip of feathers.

**precarious** (adj): uncertain; dangerous.

**R.**

**raiment** (n): clothes.

**replenish** (v): to fill up again.

**reprisal** (n): repetition of an act; retaliation.

**reservation** (n): land set aside for Indians.

**reserve** (v): to set aside or apart; to save up for the future; to book something e.g. a table at a restaurant.

**review** (v): to examine critically. A 'reviewer' is someone who writes reviews of books, plays, movies, etc.

**rivet** (n): a bolt used for fastening metal plates.

**S.**

**scheme** (n): plan.

**shears** (n): a large scissors-like instrument for clipping.

**shimmer** (v): to glisten; gleam.

**sieve** (n): a utensil used for sifting (flour, etc.).

**snarl** (v): to show teeth and growl.

**sombrero** (n): a broad-brimmed hat (Mexican).

**somersault** (n): a head-over-heels leap.

**stark** (adj): stiff; harsh. starkness (n). starkly (adv).

**T.**

**tarnish** (v): to lose colour (from contact with air).

**tawny** (adj): of light-brown colour.

**temperate** (adj): moderate (in temperature/climate).

**thicket** (n): a thick clump of trees or bushes.

**tradition** (n): long-standing custom.

**trowel** (n): a flat tool used for plastering cement, and in gardening.

**tundra** (n): treeless region with Arctic climate.

**V.**

**vermin** (n): troublesome insects and animals (fleas, rats etc.).

**W.**

**wade** (v): to walk through water.

**wholesome** (adj): healthy.

**writhe** (v): to twist (in pain).

# Puzzles

You can use words to create hidden meanings. Try to solve these puzzles, then make up your own.

 **First work out this riddle.**

In the mountains I am young,
In the valleys I am old,
When I reach the sea,
My blood runs cold.
What am I?

 **Choose one of the following and think of your own riddle.**

a swan    a computer   a key      a kaleidoscope

 **Puns.**

A pun is created when we play with homophones
(words that sound the same but are spelled differently and have
different meanings). Jokes are often made using puns.

1. Read the following jokes and write down the homophones that are being used.
   What do you call a juicy sock? One of a pear!
   When does a window get rattled? When it's in pane!
2. Think of as many homophones as you can and make up your own jokes using puns.

 **Jumbled words.**

Sort out these sporting puzzles and write them out. Use the clues to help you.
   1. telba netnis      (A table for two)
   2. srednour         (Make a circle)
   3. giniks           (Keep warm)
   4. snyvkidig        (Reach for the sky)

Choose a topic and make up four of your own.

# HOME
# HAIRSTYLING
# MADE EASY

## A STEP-BY-STEP GUIDE TO
## GREAT LOOKING HAIR

HAMLYN

First published in 1992 by Paul
Hamlyn Publishing Limited, part of
Reed International Books Limited,
Michelin House, 81 Fulham Road,
London SW3 6RB

Copyright © GE Fabbri 1992

ISBN 0 600 57561 6 (hardback)
ISBN 0 600 57562 4 (paperback)

A catalogue record for this book is
available from the British Library.
..............................................................

# CONTENTS

**H**ow many times have you wondered how to get your hair looking the way you want it to? **HOME HAIRSTYLING MADE EASY** answers all your styling queries from techniques to great new ideas. Here in one fact-filled, lavishly illustrated book is the information you need to keep your hair, and your man's hair, in tiptop condition.

Our **BASIC HAIRCARE** quiz is designed to help you work out your hair type and the best ways to cope with it. Your face shape can make all the difference to the hairstyle you choose, so compare your face shape with our simple guide and you won't go wrong. You can find information on the right way to wash your hair, step-by-step to conditioning and advice on how to trim your hair and solve problems such as split ends.

A great way to beautiful hair is to know how to use accessories. Follow our advice in **YOUR ESSENTIAL KIT** and find out how best to use YOUR hairstyling accessories.

There's more to drying your hair than you think. Check out the facts on scrunching and other drying methods in **DRYING TECHNIQUES** . Ever puzzle over what to use on your hair? We give you the lowdown in **MOUSSE, GEL, WAX & SPRAY,** what the products are and how to use them.

Finally, ring the changes with your hair without going to the hairdresser. Whatever the length of your hair, in **SIMPLE STYLES** there are suggestions for you to try. Our illustrated, step-by-step instructions make any style easy and you can create a *new you* in a very short time.

**HOME HAIRSTYLING MADE EASY** answers all your questions, gives you tips and advice and helps you to get the best results with your hair - and it allows you to do it all in your own home!

......................................................................

# BASIC HAIRCARE

**Expert know-how to keep your hair in great condition**

# KNOW YOUR HAIR

**How much do you really know about your hair? You probably think you know if it's dry or greasy, but there's a lot more to learn. And it's worth knowing, because the key to successful styling is knowing what you will, or more importantly won't be able to do with your hair**

Read through the questions below and either tick the answer which best describes your locks, or put your hair through a series of simple tests. Then check your score to discover your hair type and how it should be treated so it always looks good.

## CAN YOU HANDLE IT?

**When you wash your hair and then dry it naturally, what happens to it? Does it:**
Hang down without any shape or movement? ☐
Have natural wave or curl? ☐
Look full of life and bouncy? ☐
Look wiry? ☐

**When your hair's just been washed and is still wet, pull out a single hair, taking care not to stretch it. Lie the hair on a flat surface, like a mirror, and leave it to dry without touching it. Once dry, has it:**
Stayed completely straight? ☐
Curled around slightly? ☐
Twisted like a corkscrew? ☐

*Watchpoint*

*When pulling out a hair, try to hold it as close to your scalp as possible and pull sharply. Don't twist as you pull as this will distort the hair.*

**Take a smooth roller and when you've washed your hair, wind a few strands around the roller.**

**Then leave it to dry naturally. How long does it take for the curl to drop out?**
Less than a day ☐
A couple of days ☐
About a week ☐

**On average, how long would you say you spend getting your hair the way you want it in the morning?**
5 minutes or less ☐
10 minutes ☐
15 minutes ☐
20 minutes or more ☐

**Does your hair have static? In other words, does it ever lift up and follow the comb as you move it away?**
Yes ☐
No ☐

**Would you describe your hair as having a mind of its own?**
Yes ☐
No ☐

**Does your hair stand up a little at the roots?**
Yes ☐
No ☐

**Can you run your fingers through your hair to freshen up the style?**
Yes ☐
No ☐

## RESULTS

**YOU SCORED MOSTLY ☐**
**You're lucky! Your hair is easy to handle and tends to do what you tell it. But you've still got to treat it right, because it'll soon become unmanageable if you don't!**
● Choose products to suit your hair type: dry, oily, normal, permed or coloured.
● Try different ways of styling your hair – blow-dry, finger-dry, and use tongs.

**YOU SCORED MOSTLY ☐**
**Your hair isn't all that easy to handle so there's no point in attempting the impossible. The trick is to go with what you've got, rather than try to force it into a style it doesn't want to stay in.**
● Go for either short or long styles, mid-length is always more difficult to look after.
● Try setting the hair on rollers then blow-drying it as you brush your hair afterwards.
● Buy some gel/mousse/wax and try it out when you next style your hair – it may help you to control it better.

# GREASE IS THE WORD

**Brush your hair back from your face and look at it closely in the mirror. Tick the answer which best describes how it looks:**

The whole length of the hair is dull, with no sheen at all. ■

The whole length of the hair seems to be glossy. ■

The roots look shiny but the ends are dull. ☐

**With the hair still held back, smooth your fingers along the length, working away from your face. How does it feel?**

Slightly springy? ☐

Rough to touch? ■

Smooth and slippy? ■

**Wash and dry your hair as usual, but don't use any conditioner or styling products, like mousse or spray. In the evening, split a tissue in half so that it's only one layer thick and gently hold it against your scalp. Can you see any trace of oil left on the tissue:**

On the first evening? ■

**If not, don't wash your hair and try again. Can you see oil:**

On the next evening? ■

On the following morning? ■

On the third evening? ☐

On the fourth morning? ☐

On the fifth evening? ■

## RESULTS

**YOU SCORED MOSTLY** ■

**Your hair probably feels dry and coarse, can be hard to comb and tends to lack lustre and shine.**

**You're often disappointed because it looks dull, can be flyaway and prone to damage – especially split ends.**

● Don't be scared to wash your hair every day, providing you use the right type of shampoo it will not make it any drier – it may even help. Massage will help the natural oils to move down the hairshaft.

● Use a rich, cream shampoo but only give your hair one wash. Condition every time, using a preparation formulated for dry, damaged hair. If your hair's long, comb through to the ends and try to leave the conditioner on for at least a minute. Use an intensive conditioning treatment at least once a month, and try to leave it on for 30 minutes.

● Leave your hair to dry naturally whenever possible. Treat very gently when wet and only ever use a wide-toothed comb. Always use a styling mousse (or a heat styling lotion) with added conditioners before blow-drying, and keep your dryer on a low setting.

● Take vitamin B or brewer's yeast tablets every day to help encourage a healthy shine (vets give it to dogs for dull coats!)

**YOU SCORED MOSTLY** ■

**Your hair tends to look flat, lank and doesn't hold a style very well. This is often due to upset hormones – oily hair is usually worse during a person's teens and early twenties, as well as before periods.**

● Wash your hair every day – oily hair tends to pick up more dirt than other types and can smell, but don't massage too much as it increases the oils. Special shampoos are available which dry up the oils. Don't use hot water as it's thought to encourage the sebaceous glands to produce more oil.

● You probably don't need a conditioner after every wash, unless your hair is long. If it is, use a conditioner from the mid-

---

# A QUESTION OF CONDITION

**Pull a single hair from your head, hold it up to the light and examine it closely. Are there any flimsy bits peeling away about half way up the hair?**

Yes ■

No ☐

**Does the end of the hair look blunt and the same thickness as the rest (as opposed to getting thinner and tapering off)?**

Yes ■

No ☐

**How often do you use heated styling appliances, like tongs, crimpers or heated rollers?**

Every day ■

Every couple of days ■

About once a week ☐

For the odd special occasion ■

**How often do you have a perm, highlights or permanent colour?**

Never? ■

Very occasionally? ■

Often – more than three times a year? ■

**Do you use conditioner:**

Every single time that you wash your hair? ■

Every now and then? ■

Never? ■

**Put a ruler on the table. When your hair's freshly washed and still wet, pull out a single hair and hold it firmly at one end of the ruler. Gently stretch the hair by pulling the other end. Does it:**

Stretch about one third or more of its original length? ■

Break before it reaches one third? ■

**Do you use an intensive, or special conditioner:**

Once a week? ■

About once a month? ■

Only ever once or twice? ■

Never? ■

**When you study a strand of your hair, do the roots look shiny but the ends of your hair look dull?**

Yes ■

No ■

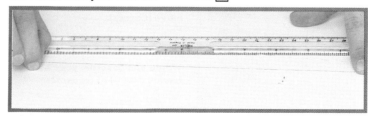

---

# RESULTS

**YOU SCORED MOSTLY** ■

**Your hair isn't in brilliant condition. It's probably difficult to comb when it's wet, and has a tendency to tangle. It feels coarse, and can look slightly fuzzy and matt – it won't have much shine.**

● Use a conditioner every time you wash your hair, to help put back the shine and make it more manageable. Choose the one that best suits your hair type: frequent-use lotions are best for oily hair: normal hair creams for dry, colour-treated or permed hair.

● Use an intensive (oil or wax based) conditioning treatment twice a month.

● Spray-on conditioners that aren't washed out are great for dry ends and give a boost to curls and perms in particular.

length to the ends only, and avoid putting any on your scalp.
● Don't overload your hair with lots of dirt-attracting styling products. Choose layered styles, rather than one-length, because they're easier to add body to and won't look so limp. Avoid fringes and styles which leave hair around your face.
● Use spirit-based conditioning lotions to dry up the oils.

**YOU SCORED MOSTLY** ☐
**You're lucky, you've got the easiest type of hair to deal with and it suits most styles. Your**

Take care not to use too much if you've got very fine hair, and unless your hair is very thick, don't use them very close to the scalp.
● Always use a heat styling lotion or styling mousse before blow-drying to help protect your hair from the heat of the dryer. Don't use heated stylers too often and check your brushes and combs regularly for rough edges that may split and tear your hair.
● If you've got long hair that's dry at the ends, use one of the dry ends creams. These have an extra thick formulation, which you just put onto the bottom couple of inches of hair to condition it.
● Avoid perming or chemical colouring treatments: they won't help your hair's condition at all. Go for vegetable colours, especially shades of red, and

hair looks shiny, without having particularly oily roots or over-dry ends.
Wash your hair as often as it needs it. Use a frequent-wash shampoo – you'll only need to wash your hair once.
Use a conditioner as needed, but if you've got long hair be sure to use it at least on the ends – they'll be a bit drier than the rest. And if your hair ever feels tangled or is hard to comb when wet, you must use a conditioner.
Try a spray-on conditioner that you don't wash out after applying. A light formulation won't overload your hair.
Treat yourself to an occasional deep conditioning treatment to maintain the texture and shine.
Normal hair is usually quite strong, so it takes colouring and perming well. But if you want it to stay normal, don't subject it to more than three chemical treatments a year. Opt for vegetable-based colours not chemically based and always test before next chemical/vegetable treatment.
Don't use heated styling products too often.

natural rinses to make your hair look shiny.

**YOU SCORED MOSTLY** ☐
**Your hair's in good shape. It looks healthy and shiny, and will take colour or perms well. But don't be complacent, it'll soon go out of condition if you don't keep up the good work:**
● Use conditioners regularly – the right one for your hair type when you wash, and an intensive conditioning treatment once a month.
● Trim your hair regularly – this will help keep the style, and make sure you never suffer from split ends.
● Don't overdo the permanent colour or perms – if you do use chemical treatments on your hair, make sure it's less than three times a year.
● Check that the shampoo you're using isn't too harsh.

# IS IT THICK OR THIN?

**Pull out a long hair and tightly wind it along an orange stick for about 2 mm. Then count how many times it'll wrap around.**
Up to 15? ☐
16-30? ☐
31 and over? ☐

**Pull out another hair. Hold it between your finger and thumb, leaving about 2-3 cm/¾-1¼ in sticking out. Does it:**
Bend over the side without any natural support? ☐
Stand up straight? ☐
Support itself for about 1 cm/⅓ in before bending? ☐

**Sit in front of a mirror with the light, preferably daylight, behind you. Part your hair down the middle and take hold of a few hairs – about 1 cm/⅓ in square. Lift them straight up by holding the ends of the hair. Does the hair look:**

So tightly packed together that you cannot see through it? ☐
Quite transparent and easy to see through? ☐

Difficult to see through. It parted easily, but no light seems to be shining through your hair? ☐

# RESULTS

**YOU SCORED MOSTLY** ☐
**Lots of people envy someone with very thick hair, but you know how annoying it can be. The trick is not to fight your hair's natural movement – make the most of its natural texture and accept that it'll never look really smooth and sleek. Although your hair's likely to be quite resistant to colours and perms, which means the processing might take longer, the results are always worth it because they tend to last longer on thick hair than on any other hair types.**
● Stick to short styles. If you like your hair long, stick to one-length styles, or ones with long layers (short layers tend to stick out).
● Go for techniques like scrunching and fingerwaving.
● Coarse hair needs regular conditioning to prevent it looking frizzy. Pick the right products to suit your hair type.

**YOU SCORED MOSTLY** ☐
**Your hair tends to look limp very quickly, so regular trims are a must to keep it in shape. Choose a style that needs minimum attention – a short crop or one-length bob are both ideal. Your hair will look thicker if it swings free of your shoulders, so unless you really love long hair, keep it at jaw level or above.**
● Consider highlights, they will help to add texture and body to your hair. All-over lighteners aren't a good idea because fine hair tends to be delicate and susceptible to damage.
● Avoid all-over curly perms. If your hair's at all fragile they may encourage it to break or go frizzy. But a body or root perm will work well.
● Use a heat styling lotion or mousse before you style – thin hair is particularly prone to flyaway ends.

A good hairstyle is all about disguising your bad points and playing up your good. You probably feel quite familiar with the face that stares back at you every morning, but try asking a handful of friends what shape they think it is and you're likely to get a handful of answers. The best way to find out is to test its shape yourself. Your face should fall into one of five basic categories: oval, round, square, heart-shaped or long. If you've got an oval face aren't you the lucky one because any style should suit you. If you haven't, then you'll need to spend a little time finding a hairstyle that makes the most of your face.

Square-shaped faces *are complemented by wavy hair which frames them.*

Heart-shaped faces *look best with shorter hairstyles which emphasise the smallness of the chin.*

# FACE VALUES

Long-shaped faces *call for short, wide hairstyles to balance their length.*

Round-shaped faces *need simple hairstyles to frame them and give the impression that they are smaller.*

# TRACE YOUR FACE

*Probably the easiest and most effective way to find your face shape is to scrape your hair from your face (use a hairband or scarf if necessary) and look closely in a well-lit mirror. Then using a lipstick or a soft eye pencil, draw a line on the mirror around the outline of your reflection. When you stand away from the mirror you'll be able to see which category your face shape falls into.*

# FACE ACHES

Learn how to disguise your own particular problem area.

- Big ears: choose a style that gives volume at the sides.
- Big nose: opt for a layered fringe and softly layered styles to draw attention away from it.
- High forehead: never style hair away from face. Instead opt for a full or layered fringe.
- Low forehead: avoid emphasising your forehead with an off-the-face style. Go for a full fringe instead.
- Double chin – there's no need to cover up with polo necks and scarves – choose a style that falls onto your face and that isn't cut above chin level.
- Eyes close together: try to avoid styles with a heavy fringe. Instead go for an upswept look. that's styled away from the face.
- Small face: don't overwhelm delicate features. Wear your hair off your face and style it to give height on top and plenty of volume at the sides.

| FACE SHAPE | CHOOSE | AVOID |
|---|---|---|
| **Heart –** wide cheekbones and a broad forehead tapering down into a small, often quite pointed, chin. | Wavy or straight short bobs. Short and spiky styles. Unstructured, wispy fringes will divert attention away from wide foreheads. | Any style with a middle parting or a very short fringe. They will make your forehead look even broader. |
| **Square –** doesn't mean that you've got a face like Frankenstein's, but that you've got a fairly broad jawline that is often squarish in shape and roughly the same width as your cheekbones. | Wavy or curly styles. Styles that are dried falling onto the face. Side partings. Fringes combed away from the face – these are the perfect complement to this face shape. | Geometric shapes. Long bobs with heavy fringes. Very short cuts. Severe styles where hair is scraped off the face and centre partings. |
| **Long –** generally with a long chin or a high forehead. | Styles with fringes to shorten the effect of a long face. Chin-length scrunch-dried or curly bobs that'll balance a long face. | Long, straight, one-length styles. Styles pulled severely off the face. These will only draw attention to your chin and forehead. |
| **Round –** the cheeks are the widest part of the face. Having a round-shaped face needn't mean you are overweight. | Unfussy styles with height on top. Bobs that are flicked out below jawline. Styles worn on the face. Side partings. | Bubbly perms and ringlets. Swept-back styles. These have the effect of making the face look rounder. |

# SHAPE UP

*The shape of your face is one of the most important considerations when choosing a new hairstyle, but you should also take into account your overall body shape.*

- *Traditional English pear-shapes should not go for cropped elfin styles or anything similar. They will only draw attention to the bottom half of your body – making your head look small for your body and your hips even wider.*
- *Big-busted girls should also avoid very cropped styles and go for a full head of hair instead. Unless, or course, you want to draw attention to your chest!*
- *Very petite girls should try to avoid having masses of very curly hair – it'll probably make your head look too big for your little body!*

**Is your hair dry and frizzy, and looks beyond repair?**

**Then treat it to a new hi-tech conditioner and**

**get it super soft and shiny in a flash!**

# HAIR SAVERS

Modern styling techniques can take their toll on the look and feel of your hair. Even if you make the effort to slap on a generous blob of conditioner after every shampoo, it's not always enough to correct the damage that's been done. Therefore, it's a good idea to switch to one of the hair-saving conditioners which are specially formulated to coat the hair shaft and leave you with hair that's beautifully manageable and silky smooth.

Follow our guide to the best products around and choose the one that's most suitable for your type of hair.

## HOT OIL

This treatment revitalises dry, brittle hair, protects it against further damage, and is the ideal solution for fragile, permed or coloured hair.

Since the oil treatment is used before shampooing, it won't leave a greasy residue. Everyone will benefit from a once a month treatment, but if your hair is badly damaged, you should use it as often as once a week.

▶ **Put an unopened tube of hot oil treatment into a cup of hot tap water for a minute or two to warm up.**

▼ **Snap open the top of the tube and spread the oil, as evenly as possible, over your hair using your fingers.**

▲ **Massage in the oil for one minute. If your hair gets greasy at the roots, concentrate on the ends. But if you suffer from a dry, itchy scalp, massage the oil in with the pads of your fingers. Shampoo as usual.**

# CONDITIONING MOUSSE

Look out for the latest conditioning mousses, which are suitable for all hair types. They tend to be fairly cheap to use since you can accurately control how much you need and where you want the mousse to go. The advantage of conditioning mousse is that it doesn't have to be rinsed out and many contain a built-in sunscreen to help prevent your hair drying out. The foam is light and can be used both to condition your hair and control it if it's flyaway.

▶ **Wash your hair and towel-dry it. Make sure you rinse your hair properly so there's no shampoo left in it.**

▼ **Shake the can of mousse and squirt a blob into your palm – use an egg-sized blob on short to mid-length hair; an orange- to grapefruit-sized blob on longer styles. If you're just conditioning the ends of your hair, go for an egg-sized blob.**

## COMB OUT

*The whole business of shampooing and massaging in conditioners can leave some nasty tangles in your hair. Rinsing won't remove these knots and by the time you come to styling your hair, you could damage it by having to tug at the tangles. That's why it's a good idea to comb your hair while the conditioner is still in it. This not only makes it more manageable and easy to style afterwards but it also distributes the conditioner, so it coats each strand evenly. Remember, however, to use a wide-toothed comb. Hair is not very elastic when it's wet and may snap, instead of springing back, if it's stretched by a fine-toothed comb.*

▲ **Smooth the mousse between your hands and massage it through your hair from the roots to the ends. Then comb it through with a wide-toothed comb. It'll form a protective coating on your hair and encourage gloss and shine.** ▶

# CREAM CONDITIONER

These are great pick-me-ups for dry hair. But their rich, waxy consistency may leave fine hair lank and lifeless. They can be used as often as you need – even after every shampoo – until your hair improves.

*Be generous with the conditioner and use plenty to cover your hair.*

**Shampoo your hair then comb through a cupful of conditioner. Leave on for three to five minutes then rinse out.**

# SUPER SERUM

Serums are the latest products on the market designed to deal with dry, split ends. The soft, liquid gel dissolves into an oil conditioner that is massaged into the ends of the hair only. It's claimed that the serums form a delicate film around dry, brittle ends, allowing the active ingredients to moisturise, strengthen and even rebuild the hair tips! The serum doesn't need to be rinsed out and is non-sticky and non-greasy. It leaves hair shiny and easy to style. It's best used twice weekly.

▲ **Brush your hair through to remove any tangles.**

◄ **The serum can be put on either dry hair or slightly damp, towel-dried hair.**

► **Squeeze out a pea-sized blob of serum and run it between your fingertips until it turns into a liquid gel. Then massage it into the ends of your hair.**

◄ **If your hair is already dry, simply style it into place. But if it's only towel-dried, blow-dry and style your hair as usual.**

*If your hair is curly use a serum designed for it, they tame frizz and make it manageable.*

Many other intensive conditioners are made from natural ingredients, such as henna, wax, seaweed or mud. These contain proteins and minerals which are claimed to strengthen the hair shaft. They need only be used occasionally.

# THE GREEN ALTERNATIVE

▲ **Start by giving your hair a good brush through to get rid of any tangles.**

◄ **Scoop out a generous handful of the conditioner and massage it into your scalp, as well as your hair, since the herbal ingredients can treat scalp problems too.**

► **As the conditioner has to be left on on for 30 minutes, or more if possible, it's best to gather up your hair on the top of your head. The thick consistency of the conditioner will keep it plastered in place. But if your hair is very long, try tucking it under a plastic shower cap.**

► **When the time's up, rinse out the conditioner, then shampoo your hair as usual. If your hair is very dry follow with a light conditioner which can be rinsed out.**

# 'HELP I CAN'T DO A THING WITH MY HAIR'

**Split ends? Dry hair? Growing out a perm?**

**Don't despair – try our instant and long-term**

**solutions to make your hair a shining example**

## SPLIT ENDS

*'I've not taken proper care of my hair and now I've got really bad split ends. What should I do about them?'*

### Tip

*Long hair is often lighter at the ends if you've spent time in the sun. An upswept style creates a flattering contrast between light ends and dark roots.*

### SHORT TERM

*Keep them out of sight in a bun or a French pleat where all the ends are covered. Avoid voluminous, curled styles which can emphasise the bushy appearance of split ends.*

### LONG TERM

*There is only one way to get rid of split ends and that's with a regular trim every six weeks. Avoid creating more splits by learning to blow-dry your hair in sections, with the dryer pointing downwards. This technique* smooths the cuticle so that your hair looks its shiny best and can protect itself from further damage.

Also, don't hold the dryer too close to your hair, since it can cause it to dry out and make the ends split. Let your hair dry naturally as often as possible and when putting it up, don't pull it or twist it too tightly. Never use ordinary elastic bands, covered ones are much gentler.

## GROWING OUT COLOUR

*'I had my hair coloured two months ago and now it's two-toned. How can I cover up the different shades?'*

### SHORT TERM

*Hide your roots! Try a high ponytail or a tousled bun so the length of your hair is piled up on top of your head. Layered looks also help to break up contrasts in colour whereas sleek smooth ones show them off – so choose a style with care.*

### LONG TERM

*If you want to stay the same colour, ask your hairdresser to retouch your roots. To grow the colour out, ask for the ends to be dyed back to your natural shade. A short, layered style breaks up the colour differences.*

# GROWING OUT LAYERS

'I'm trying to grow out my layers, but my hair looks a mess. What can I do about it?'

## SHORT TERM

Make the most of your hair's volume so that you have a full look without sharp, neat edges which would emphasise the layers. Tip your head forwards and dry your hair so that you create root lift and a tousled effect, or try scrunch-drying to make soft curls. Long fringes can be dried away from your face and secured with a slide or back-combed and worked into the rest of your hair.

## LONG TERM

Regular trims are essential to even up the layers and to allow your hairdresser to start shaping your hair, as it grows, into the new style you'll eventually have – it'll stay tidier too. The growing-out period may be slightly longer than if you leave your hair to do it's own thing, but it will look much better.

# THIN HAIR

'My hair is very fine and straight, so any style I try flops quickly. It just seems to go flat whatever I do. Please help me!'

## SHORT TERM

You can add a certain amount of temporary body to fine hair by working mousse or thickening lotion through your hair before blow-drying it and then finishing with a spritz of firm-hold hairspray. Make the most of smooth, sleek styles or try sweeping your hair into a loose bun, French pleat or high ponytail on top of your head.

## LONG TERM

You can't, of course, change the texture of your hair, but a good cut can help. Long layers can create body at the ends of your hair, while short layers can add lift to the roots. If you want curl as well as volume, try a root perm on shorter hair, or a body perm on longer.

# OLD PERM

'How can I cope with my frizzy, growing-out perm ends and new 'flat' roots?'

## SHORT TERM

After washing and conditioning your hair, work in an orange-sized blob of mousse then scrunch-dry the ends to shape and boost the curls for the rest of the day. Add height to straight roots by sweeping your hair up at the front and securing it with a slide. Also, look out for products designed to revive curls. There are ranges available that contain shampoo, mousse and hairspray.

## LONG TERM

A second full perm is out of the question because the ends will be too fragile and could break, so opt for a roots-only treatment. A root perm is more gentle and will bring back the effect of your original look by lifting and curling the new hair.

### Watchpoint

If you want to grow out an old perm, don't neglect your hair since the treated ends can split very easily. Instead, go for a smart, shorter look, then your hairdresser can cut off the untidy permed hair.

# OILY HAIR

'My hair is oily and I don't have the time to wash it every day to keep it looking at its best. Any suggestions?'

## SHORT TERM

If you are going out straight from the office, try to style your hair as simply as possible, since too much brushing and handling spreads the oil.

Dab a few drops of cologne along your parting or around the hairline where oiliness shows most clearly – the alcohol will dry up some of the oil, and the scent will mask the smoky smells that tend to stick to oily hair. You could also try using a dry shampoo which will absorb some of the oil, but make sure you brush it all out thoroughly.

## LONG TERM

Oily hair is caused by over-active sebaceous glands which produce the hair's natural lubrication, sebum, and is most common during puberty. The best remedy is to keep yourself really fit so your body can cope with any changes. Try to exercise regularly, have early nights, avoid smoking and drinking, and eat healthily.

# THICK HAIR

'I have long, thick hair and even combing it can be a problem, let alone styling or shaping it. Can you help me?'

## SHORT TERM

Don't attempt fussy styles, instead take full advantage of your hair's natural volume and go for sweeping looks.

If you fancy an elegant style for evenings, use a little gel to smooth down the roots and then simply plait or twist it up into a bun. Or braid your hair into a thick plait and decorate it with a scrunchie.

## LONG TERM

Careful cutting and layering can thin out thick hair. Alternatively, go for a style that depends upon the hair's weight to look good – a blunt-cut bob, a long, tousled look or a graduated cut, for instance. If your hair tends to fall over your face, ask your hairdresser to create a feathered face-framing style for you.

Very thick hair tends not to reflect much light, so brighten it up with a temporary colourant in a rich shade which complements your own hair colour.

# DRY HAIR

'My hair is dull and dry. What can I do to get it looking shiny and healthy again?'

## SHORT TERM

Make sure you always rinse your hair thoroughly to remove any traces of shampoo. Avoid styling products that dull the surface of your hair – mousse and hairspray can both cause problems, and switch to products that shine as they style – wet-look gel and wax are good to use.

Use a mild, frequent-use shampoo so you don't strip the hair of natural oil and follow with a rich, creamy conditioner.

## LONG TERM

If your hair is only dry at the ends it probably just needs trimming and could benefit from using a nourishing conditioner twice weekly. A hormone imbalance at certain times of the month can sometimes cause dryness. So if your hair is dry all over, you should be careful about your diet. Eat lots of fresh fruit and vegetables as well as nuts, pulses and yeast foods which are rich in the healthy hair vitamins B and C. Also, stimulate the circulation by massaging your scalp thoroughly and regularly with your fingertips.

Photographs: PAUL MITCHELL/Hair: JUSTIN/Make-up: KARIN DARNELL/Blue top: DAMART/Orange T-shirt: ZOO Earrings: ACCESSORIZE/White sweater: WAREHOUSE/Earrings: ACCESSORIZE/Green T-shirt: TOP SHOP/Black dress: ZOO/Earrings: ZOO/Earrings: C17/Earrings: ACCESSORIZE

# THE RIGHT SHAMPOO FOR THE JOB

It's important that you know your hair type if you want to get the best results possible from your shampoo.

*If you have been using styling products that aren't water soluble, like waxes, put the shampoo on your hair before you wet it. By doing this, you will emulsify the oils before you start washing and make any styling products a lot easier to remove.*

### NORMAL HAIR

This is healthy and manageable. If it's fine, it may have quite a lot of static.

Use a mild shampoo formulated for frequent use and look out for shampoos with added ingredients like grapefruit or lemon which have a slightly astringent quality and will clean and refresh your scalp.

*Two-in-one shampoo and conditioners are ideal for normal hair that doesn't need a great deal of conditioning. They can also make normal hair a lot easier to comb through after washing if it's prone to tangles and knots.*

### DRY HAIR

This hair type tends to look dull, coarse and lack-lustre and if it's long it will probably have split ends. It is often quite unmanageable and prone to static. The scalp may also be dry and flaky. Dry hair needs washing carefully as it is particularly vulnerable to damage. Choose a rich, cream shampoo with conditioning ingredients like jojoba oil. You'll only need a small blob of shampoo – just concentrate on the scalp, not the ends and rinse thoroughly. Remember, just because your shampoo produces lots of lather, this doesn't mean the shampoo is any more effective or richer. Manufacturers often add lathering agents to shampoos because most people think that more lather means cleaner hair.

*If your hair is very dry, massage your scalp with warm almond oil before you shampoo – this stimulates blood circulation and acts like a protective coating for the scalp and roots. Then apply a mild shampoo and rinse off as usual.*

### COMBINATION HAIR

This is a common problem for long hair and means that your hair is oily at the scalp and dry at the ends. Use a mild shampoo that cleans gently, removing oil from the scalp without overdrying the ends. Hair that's prone to oiliness becomes oilier and more limp as the weather warms up so you may have to wash it more in the summer.

*If your hair is below shoulder length, never pile it up on top of your head while you're washing or you'll be asking for a mass of tangles.*

### GREASY HAIR

This is lank, dull and difficult to manage. It clings to the scalp and sometimes smells as it traps sebum, sweat and dirt. The greasies are most common during adolescence when the sebaceous glands are over active and provide too much natural oil (sebum). Unfortunately there is no way of curing over-active sebaceous glands, you'll just have to wash more often. As a temporary measure, stop your scalp and hair smelling by cutting up a lime into slices and rubbing it over your hair and scalp.

# WASHING ROUTINE

**1** Brush your hair through thoroughly to get rid of tangles and loosen any dead skin cells on your scalp. Soak your hair with warm water using a shower attachment.

**4** Rinse your hair in warm water, don't stop until the water going down the drain is completely clear.

*Always rinse your hair thoroughly – any residue of shampoo or conditioner will leave it lack lustre and dull.*

*If you suffer from dandruff, the specially formulated anti-dandruff shampoos on the market are extremely effective and should clear the problem up in a few weeks. But avoid using anti-dandruff shampoos all the time as they tend to dry out your hair. Use them once a week and alternate with a frequent use shampoo until your scalp is clear. If the problem persists, go and see your doctor.*

### SPECIAL SHAMPOOS FOR COLOURED HAIR

You can buy shampoos that are made specifically for different coloured hair. They won't actually change the colour of your hair but they should enhance its natural highlights. The henna-based ones designed for red hair tend to produce the most noticeable results.

### CHEMICALLY TREATED

If your hair has been bleached, permed, coloured or straightened choose a rich shampoo for treated hair to help keep it in good condition.

**2** Pour a dollop of shampoo that's the size of a big button into one hand then rub your palms together. This ensures the shampoo is evenly distributed instead of going on in one big blob.

**3** Using the pads of your fingers, massage the shampoo into your hair and scalp. Concentrate on your scalp and the hair nearest to it. Don't put shampoo down the length of your hair, there's no need.

**5** When you've rinsed out all the lather, give your hair a final rinse in cold water to encourage a healthy shine. Wrap your hair in a towel, turban style.

*Watchpoint*

*Do not pull or rub the hair during washing as hair is very vulnerable when wet.*

**6** Gently blot your hair dry with the towel. Don't rub or you'll end up with tangles and you risk damaging your hair.

*Tip*

*There's no need to shampoo your hair twice unless it's really greasy or dirty.*

---

*Tip*

*If your hair is chemically treated, look out for special conditioning shampoos for permed or colour-treated hair.*

**GREEN CLEAN**

If you are concerned about looking after the environment, choose a biodegradable shampoo that breaks down naturally and doesn't contain any harmful pollutants.

**USE OF DRY SHAMPOOS**

There really isn't anything to equal thorough shampooing for good looking and fresh-smelling hair. But if you really haven't got time to do this, then try a dry shampoo as a temporary measure instead.

Dry shampoos come in powder form and it's essential that they are brushed out thoroughly after use or they'll leave your scalp dry and itchy and your hair looking dull. Once you've put the powder on as instructed, spend a minute or so brushing it out. You can also use ordinary talc as an emergency alternative.

*Watchpoint*

*Never use your fingernails when massaging in shampoo or you could scratch your scalp.*

# IT JUST WON'T WASH

It is possible to leave your hair unwashed for ages and for it to still look perfectly allright. But first you need to consider your hair type and whether you can face each day, without having washed your hair.

Still, if you'd like to have a go at leaving your hair unwashed for a while, first look at your hair type. This idea works best on coarse, dry and wavy hair – fine, greasy hair doesn't look too good if left unwashed.

It may sound hard to believe but you can get away with simply massaging a little conditioner into your scalp when you feel your hair is dirty and then rinsing it away with water.

You'll also need to brush hair more regularly so you can draw oil away from the roots and loosen any dead hair.

If you decide to experiment with leaving your hair unwashed for a while, good luck, but if you find it's not working for you and your hair looks absolutely dreadful, this can be easily remedied – all you need to do is reach for the shampoo and wash your hair!

# ON THE FRINGE

A precisely cut fringe starts to lose its shape when your hair grows. Take up DIY trimming and bring your fringe back into line with a few short snips!

## BLUNT CUTS
create...

bold looks that show off both your hair and features.

**They suit:**

● Strong hair colours – such as red, dark brown and golden blonde.

● Straight, thick hair – they will emphasise the texture and condition.

● Sculptured, fine features.

● One-length hair – from a bob to waist-length!

## TEXTURED FRINGES create...

soft, romantic looks that gently frame your features.

**They suit:**

● Softer hair colours – dark blondes and mid-browns.

● Highlighted hair – the layers emphasise the colour.

● Hair that's growing out a colour or a perm – textured hair hides any strong contrast between the roots and main length.

● Layered and curly hair.

● Fine hair – texture adds body.

● Soft, rounded features.

A strong fringe shows off your features and makes your hair seem very much longer!

**BEFORE**
Start with freshly washed and dried hair. Don't use styling products since they can cause your hair to curl slightly.

## GOING STRAIGHT

Show off long, shiny hair and fine features with a blunt-cut fringe.

Brown top: ZOO

1 Comb the fringe forwards then clip the rest of your hair out of the way so you can't cut into it by accident.

**2** *Comb your fringe down flat so that you can cut your hair to an even length. To find the correct line for your fringe measure from a point halfway back to the centre of your crown and out to the edges of each eyebrow. Start trimming, with short, neat snips, at the centre of your fringe so that you've a guideline for both sides.*

**3** *Comb your fringe down after each cut to make sure the hair is flat for the next snip. Move round to the side of your fringe and trim this too.*

*Watchpoint*

*Cut your fringe when it is damp or towel-dried since wet hair hangs lower on your face.*

*Tip*

*Look straight ahead into a mirror to see what you are doing. Don't look up because you'll lift your eyebrows and make your fringe look much longer than it really is!*

**4** *Use the original centre length as a guide when you trim the other side. Then tidy up any long, straggly hairs – but go easy or you could end up with less fringe than you'd bargained for!*

**To really show off a newly-trimmed, neat fringe, take the hair away from your face and style into a beehive or a soft bun.**

SCHWARZKOPF

**BRIGHT LIGHTS** This fringe is only slightly shorter than the bob. **SUITS:** Medium to thick hair.

CLYNOL

**IN TRIM A short** wispy fringe softens this otherwise severe crop and emphasises eyes and eyebrow shape. **SUITS:** Fine to medium thick, layered hair.

CLAIROL

**GREAT FRINGE** Pick a few tendrils and cut to eyebrow length. **SUITS:** Curly hair.

**Tip**

*Holding the scissors properly gives you control. Place thumb in the bottom handle, ring finger in the top and lift your little finger up for balance!*

# SOFT TOUCH

*As a change from a straight fringe, try layering it for a much softer and more versatile finish. You won't lose out on its thickness.*

**BEFORE**
*Make sure that your hair is dry and well-combed before you begin.*

**A layered fringe softens your features. Its thicker texture adds volume and weight to your hair.**

Jacket and sweater: HENNES

ELIDA GIBBS

**AT THE FRONT** Rough-dry the fringe for plenty of movement.
**SUITS: Thick, curly hair.**

SCHWARZKOPF

**CUT SHORT** This blunt-cut fringe shows off regular features.
**SUITS: Thick, one-length hair.**

L'ORÉAL

**FRINGE FRIENDS** Team up with your man and have matching fringes for double the style!
**SUITS: Thick-textured hair with a wave.**

22

1 Carefully trim your fringe so it's level with your eyebrows. Layering will shorten it to the right length.

2 Hold the middle of the fringe at the ends and pull it up vertically. The shorter hair will fall forwards, leaving the longer length free. Trim this, from front to back, along your fingers – use this as a guide and trim the rest to match.

3 To check the fringe is straight, lift it up widthways. Hold the hair at the ends so that the shorter lengths fall forward. The line across the longer hair should be even, but trim lightly if not.

**Emphasise texture by rubbing through a marble-sized blob of mousse and blow-drying the fringe so it lies to one side.**

4 Finally, to soften the bottom of your fringe, snip vertically along the edge. Aim to reach 2.5 cm/1 in into the fringe length.

Photographs: PAUL LAWRENCE/Make-up: LIZZIE COURT/Hair: JUSTIN WILLIAMS/Pinafore and shirt: WAREHOUSE/Earrings: ACCESSORIZE

# FRINGE BENEFITS

## ON WET HAIR

- Work a pea-sized blob of gel into the roots of your fringe to spike it up high.
- Rub a marble-sized blob of mousse into the fringe and blow-dry for texture.
- Thickening lotion adds weight.
- Blow-dry your fringe straight, brushing with a round brush. For a solid look use heated straighteners.

## ON DRY HAIR

- Tease a thumbnail-sized blob of wax through your fringe to break up the volume slightly, or smooth it down the length for a solid look.
- Spritz with hairspray to create a soft flick.
- Gently back-comb the roots for height and extra volume.
- Comb through a pea-sized blob of wet-look gel for a really slick finish.

*Tip*

Naturally curly or tightly permed hair looks great with a fringe. Go for a layered fringe, or just a few strands or tendrils rather than a thick, heavy, blunt-cut, fringe.

# FRINGE FACTS

- When 'Beatle fringes' were popular in the Sixties, there was an outbreak of spots on foreheads! Don't let this happen to you – always keep your fringe scrupulously clean.
- A shorter fringe makes your face look wider and rounder. A longer fringe will give length to your face.
- Don't let your fringe hang below your eyebrows all the time. Your hair could look untidy and you risk straining your eyes!
- A slightly curved fringe flatters a long nose or a small face.

*Tip*

No time to wash your hair? Then wash just your fringe instead and let it dry naturally – a clean fringe will instantly pep up lank hair.

*Warning point*

If your parting's on the left, the left-hand side of your fringe may be slightly longer, with the reverse effect if your parting is on the right. Trim to even it up.

23

**BEFORE**
*Suggest he washes his hair first, or damp it down with a water spray.*

# GIVE HIM A TRIM

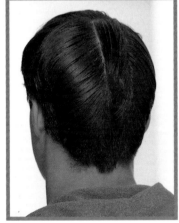

1 *Part the hair from ear to ear. Next, make two partings down the back of the head, dividing the back hair into three panels.*

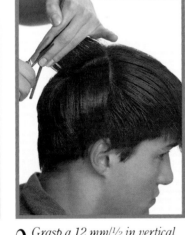

2 *Grasp a 12 mm/½ in vertical section from the top of the centre panel between your middle and index fingers, then cut.*

For most men a trip to the hairdresser or barber is a bit of a chore, however much their hair may be in need of a trim. So why not trim it yourself – it's quite easy once you know how. Although you won't be able to manage a complete restyle – that's best left to the professionals – you can

certainly give him a tidier look.

Make sure you've got plenty of time to spare – even a trim can't be rushed if you're not an expert. You'll also need a sharp pair of hairdressing scissors and, most important, a co-operative man with confidence in your ability. After all, his hair is in your hands!

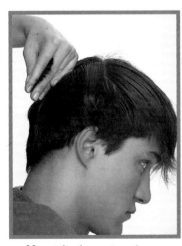

3 *Now take the next section down in the same centre panel and cut it in the same way. Continue cutting downwards.*

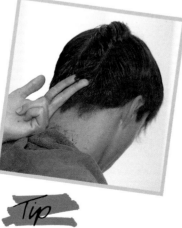

*Tip*

*To keep your hand steady when cutting the last section at the nape of the neck, rest your knuckles against his neck.*

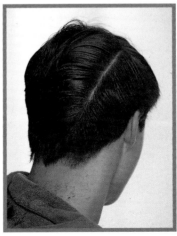

4 *Make another parting 4 cm/ 1½ in away from the previous one. Starting with the section nearest the crown, cut as before.*

5 *Now cut the section nearest the ears. Once you've completed one side of the head, cut the other in the same way.*

Photographs: STEVE SMITH/Hair: PENNY ATTWOOD/Make-up: ELLIE LEBLANC

8 *Make a further parting 4 cm/1½ in away from the previous one. Cut this section in the same way as step 7.*

9 *Make a vertical parting starting just above the ears to meet the previous parting.*

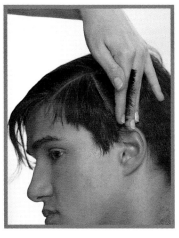

10 *Cut the back section then the front, angling your fingers downwards. Repeat steps 8 and 9 on the other side of the head.*

6 *To cut the front, make two partings down the centre in the same way as the back. You now have three front panels.*

7 *Cut the centre panel starting at the crown. Lift the hair upwards and cut at an angle to give a heavy fringe.*

# TRIMMING TIPS

● **Make sure you read through our guide thoroughly before you start. It's a good idea to run through the steps first without using scissors.**
● **Don't use any old scissors which come to hand. It's worth investing in a pair of hairdressing scissors to do the job properly. You'll find them in most major chemists.**
● **Sit your man in a chair that's the right height for you to cut his hair comfortably.**
● **Keep a water-spray handy to keep the hair damp as you cut. You'll find it's much easier for**
cutting a straight line.
● **Put a towel around his shoulders to catch the drips and snips as you cut.**
● **As a guide when you cut a new section of hair, include a few strands of hair from the previous one, so you can match the length.**
● **Comb through the section of hair before you cut so that it's smooth and tangle-free.**
● **Use hair clips if hair's long, or it won't stay out of the way.**
● **Wet shave the nape of his neck if straggly hairs are spoiling the finished hairline.**

# CUTTING KIDS' HAIR

**If your little brother or sister's in need of a trim but you know that a trip to the hairdresser will end in tears,** why not have a go yourself? Learn basic cutting and you'll keep any tearaway tidy

**BEFORE**
*Hair is definitely in need of a good trim!*

## TRIMMING LAYERS

*The simplest way to tidy up a layered cut is to start by trimming around the hairline first, then go on to trim the layers.*

Trimming a child's hair at home isn't as hard as it sounds. Once a good basic cut has been established – and a hairdresser really does have to do this – trimming it back into shape is easy. Hair needs to be neatened up every six to eight weeks, so alternate a home trim with a trip to the salon. Never try to attempt a complete re-style – this is completely different to a trim and should be left to the professionals. Just put on a favourite TV programme to distract the child and away you go!

**You need:**
*towel*
*comb*
*water spray*
*section clips*
*scissors*
*hairdryer*
*brush*
*gel*

## SCISSOR TALK

Buy a pair of *hairdressing* scissors with slightly rounded ends as these are safest for children's hair. To hold the scissors, put your thumb in the handle of the top blade, and your third finger in the handle of the bottom blade. Keeping the bottom blade still, cut with the thumb blade. Take short snips closing the blades together each time. Use only the ends of the blades to cut.

1 *Wash and towel-dry the hair, then comb it forwards from the crown and down at the sides and back.*

2 *Part the hair from just above the temples right back to the centre of the crown. Clip the rest of the hair out of the way.*

3 *Comb the fringe forwards, then take a section in the centre and cut a straight line in precise snips.*

4 *Trim both sides using the centre line as a guide. Make the fringe curve slightly downwards at the ends.*

5 Trim the sides to the same length as the fringe until you reach the top of the ear.

6 Comb the hair downwards in front of the ear and trim to form a neat triangle shape.

7 For the back, comb hair straight down, then rest the bottom blade against the neck. Start in the centre and snip towards sides.

8 Trim back corners. Comb hair downwards and continue cutting along the same line, curving slightly up above ears.

9 The napeline follows a gentle curve which suits a young child. For a sharper line, trim sides at a steeper angle.

*Tip*

Don't worry if the hair looks solid, the layers you are about to add will soften it.

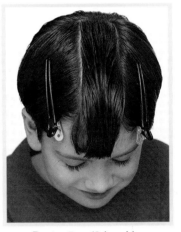

10 Part a 5 cm/2 in wide section along the top of the head and comb forwards. Clip the sides out of the way.

11 Section the hair again, this time from the crown to either side of the ears. Section the back hair to the nape.

# TRIM TIPS

● Before cutting, go through the steps without scissors to feel how the hair lies.

● Hair looks shorter when it dries, so cut the fringe slightly longer than you want.

● Always hold a cut section and a long section together as you trim so that you get an even result.

● Trim layers to the same length by holding the hair at 90° to the head.

● Make sure the child is sitting up straight while you cut back hair or you may end up with a wavy line!

● Get the child to hold the top of his ear down while you trim above it.

12 Trim the first section from crown to fringe, lifting the hair in vertical sections.

13 Continue trimming this middle section in equal stages down to the nape of the neck.

14 Now, holding the hair vertically in your fingers, trim straight across the ear to ear section.

15 *Make a diagonal section from the crown out to the hairline and trim. Repeat in sections around the head.*

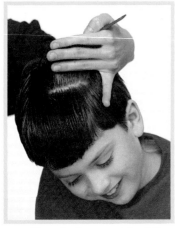

16 *Now check your cutting! Dry hair and lift a few sections across the head. If it's not all the same length, trim to even up.*

# DO'S and DONT'S

- Never cut hair in a hurry.
- Always cut hair in a good light so that you can see exactly what you're doing.
- Keep a spray of lukewarm water handy to dampen the hair if it begins to dry out.

- When cutting a fringe, hold the hair between your fingers with the finger underneath resting on the child's forehead. This will reassure the child that you are between him and the scissors!

# TRIMMING ONE LENGTH HAIR

*Whether you take off an inch or three inches the steps are the same. Allow about 45 minutes to do the job properly.*

**FINISHED**
**Blow-dry or add a little gel for a casual, spiky look.**

**BEFORE**
*A one-length cut that hasn't seen scissors for six months!*

1 *Start by washing and towel-drying the hair. Comb it straight down then part neatly in the centre.*

2 *Where the hair recedes above the temples, part the hair back to the crown. Take the centre section and trim across.*

3 *Use this first section as a guide for trimming both sides of the fringe level. Comb the fringe down and snip off any stray hairs.*

28

**4** Make a horizontal parting around the top of the child's head, then clip the top section out of the way.

**5** Comb down a 5 cm/2 in wide section of hair. Hold it between two fingers and trim along the underside taking small snips.

**6** Continue trimming all the way round cutting along the same line. Try not to lift the hair or you'll lose the line.

*Tip* Take a few steps back every now and then to double-check that you're still cutting a straight line.

**7** When you've finished trimming the underneath section it should be one even length. Trim any stray hairs.

**8** Take down the top section of hair and comb through. Trim to the same length as the underneath section.

**9** The finished cut looking nice and neat after 6.5 cm/2½ in have been cut away.

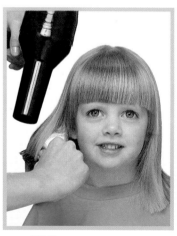

**10** While the hair is still damp, blow-dry the ends under using a round brush to soften the line.

**Choosing and using styling accessories**

# THE HEAT IS ON

**Don't be a hothead and buy the first hairdryer you set eyes on. Most of us only own one so it's worth finding out which dryer is right for your style. Get switched on with our guide to what's on offer**

One hairdryer may look pretty much like another and you may think that the only difference is in its colour or size. But hairdryers do have an amazing range of features and functions.

You'll find dryers with different speed and heat settings and a range of nozzles to suit a variety of styling techniques. They also come in various sizes. There's a number of mini-sized dryers you can take on holiday, larger professional-style ones – just like those your hairdresser uses, dryers that make very little noise and even ones that can double up as an iron!

Think carefully about what you actually want from your hairdryer before you part with your money. Will it suit your hair type? Is it the best one for making the most of your particular style? Is it small enough to fit in your suitcase and so on?

Make sure you know exactly what you're buying by reading the details on the back of the box, or the best way of all is to get a shop assistant to show you what is available.

## WHAT WATT?

**One of the most important things when buying a hairdryer is to check that the wattage (the amount of power) will suit your styling requirements. Most dryers are around 1200 watts on their highest setting but when switched to different levels of heat and speeds may be as low as 600-800 watts. Use the coolest, lowest speeds for fixing curls and setting your style and for drying permed or naturally curly hair.**

**The fastest, most powerful dryers are the professional type and these are around 1600/2000 watts. These dryers are great if you want to dry your hair quickly or your hair is long and thick. However, do take care not to use your dryer on its highest setting too often as this can damage your hair.**

**Travel dryers usually have a low wattage (600-800 watts). These are only suitable for holidays as they tend not to have enough power for everyday use.**

Hair and make-up: YA'NINA

# DRYER ROUND-UP

Check out all types of different dryers and their special features.

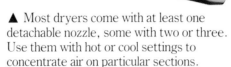

▲ Most dryers come with at least one detachable nozzle, some with two or three. Use them with hot or cool settings to concentrate air on particular sections.
**Good for:** styling small areas such as a fringe or creating small curls.

▶ A compact dryer with fold-away handle fits neatly into a suitcase. Most travel dryers are dual voltage (110/240V) so you can use them abroad.
**Good for:** taking on holidays and weekends away.

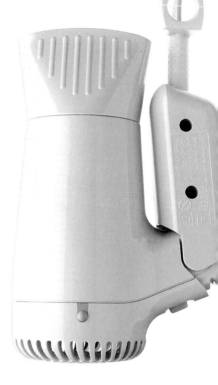

▶ A dryer with a cool setting feature. Switching from hot to cool during styling will help set your hair into shape.
**Good for:** fixing waves and curls, putting the shape back into a perm and generally creating long-lasting styles.

*Watchpoint*

*Never use your hairdryer in the bathroom or anywhere it is likely to come into contact with liquid.*

Some hairdryers are specifically designed to be quiet. Look out for words like 'low-noise'.
**Good for:** not waking the family or disturbing the neighbours when you're drying your hair or if you've got a hangover!

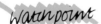

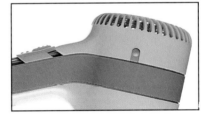

▲ **Anti-skid pads** – on the sides of dryers stop them scratching and sliding off table tops.

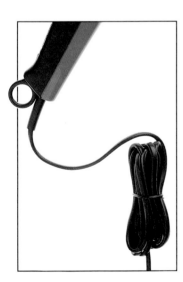

◀ **Extra long cord** – an asset if your plug socket and mirror are far apart.

▶ A diffuser is a dish-shaped attachment with prongs that you attach to the nozzle end of your dryer. It enables the air from the dryer to circulate over a wider area and is great for separating curls. It also stops your hair from drying out or frizzing.
**Good for:** permed and naturally wavy or curly styles.

# SOME LIKE IT HOT

▼ **Air filter cleaning system –** some dryers have a detachable filter at the back of the dryer which you can clean or replace.

*Watch point*

*Infra-red dryers should not be confused with ultra-violet lamps which are used for tanning. Infra-red drying is used in hairdressing salons for processing colour, perms and conditioners. It is quite safe and doesn't tan the skin.*

▲ An infra-red hairdryer is a hot, bright red lamp which dries hair with gentle heat rays rather than hot air. It dries evenly from the roots without over-drying. Comes with a stand so you don't have to hold it.
**Good for:** permed or naturally curly styles.

▶ Get two for the price of one! The hot air from this dryer heats up the iron plate and will smooth creases from all but very thick fabrics. Small enough to fit into a suitcase.
**Good for:** styling hair and ironing on holiday.

*Tip*

*If you use a hairdryer every day it's worth considering a 'professional' dryer. These are designed to withstand the rigours of continuous drying in a hairdressing salon, but they are easily obtainable for home use and should last twice as long as ordinary dryers.*

◀ This versatile professional-style dryer has a slim nozzle for concentrated drying. It's also lightweight.
**Good for:** general drying and it is especially useful if you want to blow-dry your hair straight.

▶ **Hang-up loop –** useful if you want to store your dryer neatly.

● *Always towel-dry your hair before you start blow-drying. If it's soaking wet you'll have to use the dryer for longer and you'll run the risk of damaging your hair.*
● *Never have the setting too hot and always try to hold the dryer at least 15 cm/6 in away from your hair – any closer and you could burn your hair. The exception to this rule is when you're using a diffuser attachment, which is specially designed to work close to your head.*
● *Make sure you keep the dryer moving constantly. Don't concentrate the heat on one area of hair for more than a couple of seconds at a time.*
● *First of all, rough dry your hair on a fast speed without a nozzle. Once your hair feels about half dry, switch to a slower speed then put on a nozzle for more controlled styling.*
● *Make sure your hair is completely dry, right through to the roots. If it's even slightly damp your hair will flop.*
● *Occasionally clean the mesh or vent at the back of your dryer where dust collects and replace the filter if it's removable.*

Photographs: ADRIAN TAYLOR

**Don't let styling your hair be a drag! Comb through our essential guide and get kitted out with the right tools for taming your hair**

A comb is such a basic bit of hair-care equipment that you probably use one every day and never give it a second thought. But, in fact, a comb can be an invaluable styling aid. You can use it for back-combing, blow-drying, lifting curls, making partings and for sectioning when you're winding your hair up in rollers.

In order to get the most from your style you'll probably need two or three different combs. One with widely-spaced teeth to use when your hair is wet, a tailcomb for making sections or partings, and a fine-toothed comb that you can use for back-combing when you want to add body.

# COMB TALK

● Natural materials like horn or tortoiseshell tend to be quite expensive, but are best for your hair because they don't create static.
● Avoid metal combs (these are very difficult to find these days because they are known to be so bad for your hair).
● Never use an old comb with sharp or jagged edges – since it will split and damage hair.
● Keep combs clean. Wash them frequently in warm soapy water, rinse, and leave to dry naturally.
● Be gentle when you're using a comb, especially if hair is wet.
● Move a comb down the length of your hair from the roots to the ends and then there's no reason why your style shouldn't comb up trumps!

# COMB ON

◄ **Wide-toothed comb** – widely-spaced teeth make this comb ideal for using on wet hair because it won't split or damage the hair while it's in a vulnerable state.

◄ **Afro comb** – has very long, widely-spaced teeth. These are used to lift and separate curls and are ideal for using on permed, naturally curly and Afro hair. Can also be used to comb conditioner through your hair.

▲ **Prong comb** – two combs for the price of one! A fine-toothed end for back-combing fine, straight hair and a fork-pronged end to lift and separate curly or Afro hair. Use the prong end for combing through conditioner too.

▲ **Mousse comb** – looks like a flat brush with two rows of teeth. Use it to distribute mousse or other styling products evenly through your hair – always combing from the roots through to the ends.

▲ **Baby comb** – specially designed to use on very fine, baby hair. It has softly rounded teeth that won't scratch or damage a delicate scalp.

◄ **Tortoiseshell comb** – it not only looks stylish but the wide, rounded teeth ensure that your hair can be combed when wet or dry.

# DOWN!

**▲ Perm comb** – has very short, thick, widely-spaced teeth that makes it ideal for using on all types of curly hair. A perm comb often comes with bendy rollers kits and is great for using on newly curled hair because it won't pull the curl out as a fine-toothed comb might.

*Tip*

*Don't share your comb, even with your best friend. Keep it clean and to yourself.*

**▲ Double-ended comb** – a versatile comb that has a fine-toothed end you can use for back-combing and a wider-toothed end you can use for general styling.

*Tip*

*A tailcomb with a metal handle will last longer than a plastic one – which can break easily.*

**◄ Tailcomb** – a fine-toothed comb with a long thin handle that generally tapers down to a point. It's just the thing for making neat partings, picking out sections of hair when you're winding it up into rollers, or tucking in any loose ends.

Main picture: NICK COLE/Still-life: ADRIAN TAYLOR

# HEAT WAVE

**Try out a hot brush and warm to curls and waves at the flick of a switch. You'll transform your hair into a great new style in a matter of minutes**

## WHAT'S WHAT

Hot brushes are available in several different barrel sizes. The length and density of the bristles can also vary.

Some of the latest models have interchangeable bristles to make the brush suitable for all types of hair. Here's a guide to what will give the best results.

**Choose larger bristles for:**
- Big, loose curls.
- Hair below shoulder length.
- Adding body to long hair.

**Choose small bristles for:**
- Small tight curls.
- Short hair.
- Adding body to short hair.

If your hot brush doesn't have a choice of bristles, take smaller sections of hair to make smaller curls, and wider sections for soft, body-giving waves.

**Steam heat**
The steam release button gives out a measured burst of steam each time you press it. You don't need to press it more than once for each curl.

If your hot brush doesn't have steam then hold the curl for slightly longer to give it a chance to set properly.

## LOOSE WAVES

*Tousled waves on one-length hair*

**1** Your hair should be dry and tangle free. Use the larger bristles on the brush for a loose wave.

**2** To create ringlets, separate your hair into 5 cm/2 in wide vertical sections. Wrap each section, in turn, around the barrel to within 2.5 cm/1 in of your head, winding along the length of the barrel so you end up with a roll shape.

**3** Hold the brush in place for about 30 seconds. If your hair holds a curl easily then leave it for a shorter time, if it doesn't, hold it for up to a minute. Press the curl release button and draw the brush away from your hair so that it unwinds. The curl should be tight and springy.

### Tip

*Fill the steam reservoir with water and heat the brush until the light comes on. Wind the hair up around the brush and press the cap once to release the steam.*

Bra top: KNICKERBOX/Top: PURE NEW FIONA

# THE RIGHT BRUSH

**Need a new hairbrush? There's such a big variety available now that trying to find the most suitable one for you can leave you bristling with emotion! We go through the types available with a fine tooth comb**

It's easy to get confused by all the shapes when you go into your local chemist shop to buy a new brush. But they haven't just been designed as accessories to clutter up your dressing table, brushes do all have special functions.

Generally speaking, brushes fall into two categories – there are brushes like an ordinary hairbrush that are ideal for general grooming or brushing, and then there are the more specialised brushes like the vent brush which you use for styling your hair with the help of a hairdryer.

**BRUSH WORK**
You probably possess a brush of one sort or another, but chances are you haven't kept it in tip-top condition. It may have half the bristles missing, or be dirty, or it may just have suffered years of neglect and be in a rather shabby and battered state like a favourite old teddy bear.

But whatever state the brush or brushes you have are in, you must get a good general brush that suits the texture and length of your hair. It should be made of bristles that are right for your hair type (either nylon, natural bristle, a mixture of the two or plastic).

It's no use buying the most expensive hogs' hairbrush on the market if a nylon one will suit you better. Bear in mind that **natural bristle** brushes are best suited to long straight or fine long hair. The natural bristles will help your hair to look sleek and shiny without damaging the scalp. They will also help to calm down the static electricity in your hair which is likely to make it flyaway and difficult to manage.

A **nylon and bristle mix brush** will suit you best if your hair is thick and wavy and a **nylon brush** suits most hair types and textures but is particularly good for short hair.

**Vent brushes** are simply brushes that have widely-spaced bristles or quills, and air vents to allow the hot air from your dryer to circulate and prevent your hair over-heating.

Vent brushes come in cylindrical shapes or the more common rectangular shape. The cylindrical brush works best if you have got short or mid-length hair that's a medium to thick texture. You can use it for curling your hair under or straightening it.

Simply divide your hair into sections when blow-drying, being careful not to pull the hair too tightly near the tip of the brush as it is likely to get all tangled up. Direct the heat from your dryer from roots to ends – the quills all the way round the brush should allow you to get a good tension on the hair to straighten it or curl it under. Allow each section to dry thoroughly before carefully removing the brush.

**Flat vent brushes** are great for getting natural, free-flowing effects. They are very useful if your hair has slight wave or curl because the waves will not be dragged out and pulled straight as they would be with a more traditional type of brush.

You will probably have seen **bobble-tipped** brushes in the shops. Sometimes called wet brushes, the purpose of these (often very brightly coloured) bobbly ends is to protect your hair – they won't pull it, they won't scratch your scalp and they can be used to very gently brush the tangles out of wet hair.

They are also used for general brushing and blow-drying looser styles and suit most lengths of hair except very short. Bobble-ended brushes work best on hair that is medium thick through to hair which is very thick.

**Radial brushes** are round styling brushes that are usually either plastic or a nylon and bristle mixture. These can be used to create curls on all lengths of hair and for adding style and shape to short hair.

If your hair is short and wavy use a radial brush for flicking back unruly fringes, for creating gentle curls or waves, or simply for styling.

**Shampoo brush – this is excellent for gently massaging your scalp when you're shampooing. It works well on a dry scalp.**

Tip

*Don't use a flat vent brush if you want to blow-dry your hair straight. You won't be able to get enough tension to direct your hair into a straight style.*

▲ **This vent brush has holes in the back to let hot air pass through when you are using it while blow-drying your hair.**

▲ **A baby's brush with the softest of nylon bristles – gentle enough for babies' delicate scalps yet quite sufficient for their silky strands of hair.**

▶ **A thickly-bristled styling brush, ideal for creating waves and flicks.**

Tip

*Ease out tangles from long hair using a flat backed brush. Work up from the ends to the roots.*

◀ **A bobble-tipped brush (wet brush) – the bobbles mean it can be safely used on wet hair.**

# BETTER BRUSH CARE

● Keep all your brushes and combs clean and hygienic by regular washing. Don't let all your family and friends use them.

● To keep your brushes clean remove all the clogged up hair with a comb. Use an old toothbrush to get to the base of the bristles where dirt builds up and then wash the whole brush with warm water and a little shampoo. Shake off the excess water and allow it to dry naturally.

● If you have one of those brushes that you can pull the rubber-cushioned bit out to clean it, dust a little bit of talcum powder into the runners when you put it back in after cleaning. This makes it much easier to put back together.

● Do keep an eye on all your hair equipment for signs of wear and tear. Rough edges or split quills/needles will split your hair.

● If you're blow-drying your hair, make sure the brush you're using is heat resistant. Hairdressers recount horror stories of people who have come in to have brushes literally cut out of their hair – because they have melted under the heat of the hairdryer.

● Use your hairdryer on a moderate heat, not a fierce heat. Your brush will last much longer and so will your hair!

Photographs: ADRIAN TAYLOR

▼ An ordinary flat-backed natural bristle brush – the perfect choice for long straight hair. Also good for curing static electricity.

▲ A large round styling brush with plastic bristles – ideal for blow-drying.

▼ A brush to help you look after your other brushes properly – a special cleaning brush.

*Tip*

No need to give your hair one hundred brush strokes before you go to bed. You'll only end up with greasy hair and split ends. One thorough brush-over is enough.

◄ A round styling brush – which is great for giving curl to hair when blow-drying.

▼ An all-round styling brush for blow-drying – the design makes it very easy to clean.

*Tip*

Before you part with any money, check the bristles on the brush you want to buy by pressing them into the palm of your hand to check that they're not too sharp.

# DRYING TECHNIQUES

## How to style the professional way

# AIR DRYING

**Constant blow-drying can be stressful to your hair leaving it dried out, dull and prone to split ends. Whenever possible pull the plug on your dryer and switch to natural, safe drying methods instead. You only need to use your fingers and – in an amazingly short time – any length of hair will be quite dry**

Drying your hair with your hands is not as laborious as it sounds. Using just your fingers it's possible to scrunch, lift, comb, flick and twist all lengths of hair stylishly dry. And it really doesn't take very long. If you're doing it right short hair should be dry within five minutes and long hair within a quarter of an hour. The secret is to move your hands as quickly as possible through your hair to circulate the air which does all the drying for you.

*Tip*

*Finger-drying is the best way to dry heat damaged hair, or to revive the curls in your perm.*

## MAKING WAVES

**BEFORE**
*Capitalise on the curl in bob-length hair.*

*2 Tip your head as far forwards as you can and repeatedly comb your fingers through from the roots down, moving as quickly as you can. Carry on until your hair looks dry but feels damp.*

*1 Blot your hair with a towel so that it's no longer dripping wet. Comb it back and work a ping-pong ball sized blob of mousse through the roots.*

*3 Scrunch the ends of your hair towards your head with your hands, as if you are screwing up paper. This will encourage natural waves to form. Gently brush through.*

# LONG HAIR

**BEFORE**
*Finger-drying gives body and bounce to long hair, and emphasises natural curl.*

**1** ◀ **After the final rinse, squeeze excess water off your hair with a towel so it's not dripping wet.** Achieve lift by finger-drying the roots first. Flick your fingers rapidly through, close to your scalp, until it looks dry but feels damp.

**2** ▶ **Separate your hair into six sections and twist each one into a roll around your index finger. Secure with a hair grip. Leave in place for ten minutes.**

**3** ◀ **Remove grips and relax the rolls by combing with your fingers.** Continue until you have the curl size that you want.

*When drying your hair with your fingers, try to keep your hands as relaxed as possible. You'll get more movement, and avoid aching wrists!*

## ANY QUESTIONS?

**Q** Can natural drying leave my long, curly perm too full to look good?

**A** Natural drying will always create volume through your hair, but you can control how much! Work on the ends for more fullness at the bottom than the top, concentrate on the roots for fullness throughout.

**Q** How do I know that my hair will suit natural drying techniques?

**A** The beauty of these techniques is that they suit all types of hair, and all lengths.

Of course, it's much quicker to dry short cropped hair than it is to dry a waist-length style.

**Q** I like to blow-dry my hair because it makes it shine. Can I get the same effect from natural drying?

**A** Shine is created when the cuticle on the hair shaft is made to lie flat so that light reflects off it. Blow-drying is only one way to achieve this look. For a really deep shine, condition your hair after shampooing, then dry it by rapidly brushing your fingers downwards through it.

*Use gel on short styles and mousse on longer looks to help your hair hold its curls, but if your hair is already naturally curly then you can leave out this stage.*

## TOWEL TACTICS

● *Try not to rub your hair dry with a towel – you'll lift the cuticle layer on your hair leaving it vulnerable to damage. Squeezing and blotting is kinder.*

● *If you sleep on wet hair, put a towel on your pillow to absorb any wetness.*

**AND SO TO BED . . .**
*You will not catch a cold, chill or flu from sleeping on wet hair. It's harmless!*

● *The purpose of towel-drying is to stop your hair dripping water down your back and to speed up the drying process.*

● *Always move your hands away from the roots to keep the cuticle smooth, so that your hair will look shiny.*

42

# SHORT HAIR

**BEFORE**
*Shorter hair dries quickly without help, but for a stylish look follow these three simple steps.*

**1** ◀Blot your hair with a towel to remove excess water, then work a marble-sized blob of gel through the roots to help create lift and movement.

**2** ▶ Run your fingers rapidly upwards and forwards from the roots to the ends of your hair. Do this as quickly as you can until it has dried.

**3** Bend your head forwards and spray hairspray into the roots. Stay put for one minute to give the spray time to dry and set your hair.

**NATURAL DRYING ADDITIVES**
A few extras to have at hand . . .
a towel
mousse or gel
a brush

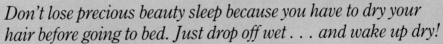

# SLEEP ON IT!

*Don't lose precious beauty sleep because you have to dry your hair before going to bed. Just drop off wet . . . and wake up dry!*

**1** *You can dry hair of any length with the aid of a thick towel. Comb wet hair and wrap it up in a towel. Overnight it will retain the heat from your head, which will gently dry your hair.*

**2** *In the morning, remove the towel and brush hair before styling.*

**1** *Long hair can be curled overnight. Pat wet hair with a towel then plait it into a French plait, so that your hair is tight at the roots. Curl the ends under into the hair-tie to avoid straight tips.*

**2** *In the morning your hair will be dry so gently release the plait and comb your fingers through to loosen the curl.*

Photographs: PAUL MITCHELL/Hair: PAULA MANN
Make-up: KAREN MASON

43

Photograph: LIZ McAULAY Hair & Make-up: YA'NINA Top: NEXT

# PUTTING ON THE SHINE

**Have you ever wondered how some people get their hair to look so wonderfully shiny? Is it completely natural or do they know something that you don't? Try these tips for no-fuss gloss**

Hair shine starts from within and your general health has a greater effect on the way it looks than you might think. Once a hair has emerged from the scalp it's effectively dead so whatever you eat can't affect the lengths – just the new growth. To ensure you're promoting healthy new hair eat a balanced diet that includes plenty of vitamin B complex, which is the most important one for shiny hair. It's no coincidence that many pet owners give it to their dogs for shiny coats!

Straight hair will always look more shiny than curly hair as its flat surface reflects light more easily. Similarly, darker hair will reflect more light than blonde hair. But don't despair if you're a curly blonde, because if you treat your hair carefully, always using conditioner after every wash and giving your hair a regular deep conditioning treatment using oil, wax or cream, you should end up with glossy locks too.

For instant shine try rubbing a fingerful of wax down the lengths of freshly styled hair – it works wonders on thick and coarse textures. But do take care to only use a little on very fine hair as it may become limp and lifeless.

Gloss sprays are perfect for all types of hair. They are simply a light oil in a spray form which coat the surface with a gentle mist without altering the shape or texture of your finished style.

Don't forget regular brushing too. While the brush goes through your hair it stimulates and distributes natural oils along the lengths and smoothes out all the tangles at the same time.

**44**

# DRYING FOR SHINE

**CHECK LIST**
Styling mousse
Hairdryer
Flat-backed or
medium-sized
round brush
Hair clips
Extras: wax,
hairspray

**1** After washing, squeeze the excess water gently from your hair with a towel. Rub too vigorously and you'll get tangles.

**2** For body and lasting hold squeeze a ball of mousse, about the size of a small egg, into the palm of one hand.

*Forget the one about giving your hair 100 strokes a day. A good brushing helps to distribute natural oils, but too many can turn your scalp into an oil slick and damage the drier ends.*

# SHINE STRIPPERS

- Blow-drying and over-use of heated styling aids.
- Rough handling, especially when hair is wet.
- Insufficient rinsing after washing.
- Chemical treatments like perming and bleaching.
- Too much strong sun.
- Overloading hair with styling products.
- Dirty brushes and combs.

**3** For maximum lift, work the mousse well into your hair, especially close to the roots. Add a little more if your hair is long.

*Watchpoint*

*Try not to use too many sticky styling products like gels and waxes, especially if you live in a city. They attract the dirt, make your hair dull and encourage grease.*

**4** Rough-dry your hair first with a dryer. This cuts down the time it will take you to blow-dry. Stop when your hair feels slightly damp.

**5** To blow-dry a smooth, sleek style use either a flat-backed or medium-sized round brush, with bristles that are fairly close together.

**6** Brush all your hair over to one side and dry a bit more. This will give your hair extra lift as you are drying it away from the direction of growth. Once finished, repeat on the other side.

**9** At the back of your head use the brush like a roller for the ends, curling the hair around it tightly while drying. For longer lasting hold leave the hair to cool for a couple of seconds before taking the brush out.

**7** To make blow-drying easier it's best to work in sections, so make a parting all the way around your head and pin the top layer of hair up out of the way. By drying the underneath layer first you can give extra volume to your chosen style.

**10** Once the bottom layer is dry, take down the rest of your hair and make a centre parting or a side parting according to your normal style.

**8** Start with the brush at the roots, then lift your hair while directing the dryer from the roots to the ends. Slowly move the brush down the length of hair holding it tightly all the time. Repeat this action all the way around using a small amount of hair at a time until it's all completely dry.

# SHINE SAVERS

● Wash your hair in warm, not hot, water. Too hot water can damage the surface of the hair, dulling natural shine. Use cool water in the final rinses.

● Avoid using heated styling appliances every day as they tend to strip your hair of natural oils, leaving it dry.

● Use a heat styling lotion before blow-drying or a styling mousse which forms a protective barrier.

● Test your hairdryer on the back of your hand. If it's too hot for your skin to bear, it will be too hot for your hair, so switch to a lower heat setting.

● Split and frizzy ends will never look shiny, so remember to get them trimmed regularly.

● If you wash your hair every day, dilute your shampoo or choose one for frequent use. Coconut shampoo is good for shine.

● Always rinse your hair in fresh water after swimming in salt or chlorinated water.

● Check all your brushes and combs regularly for signs of wear and tear. Rough edges can damage your hair.

Photographs: ADRIAN BRADBURY/Hair: PENNY ATTWOOD/Make-up: YA'NINA

**11** Start drying from the back leaving the front until last so you can match it up to the rest.

**12** Your hair looks great! It's thicker and shinier than it has ever looked before, and with practice you'll find you can dry for shine in no time at all.

# BEHIND THE SHEEN

*A healthy lifestyle will go a long way towards getting your hair fighting fit!*

● You may have read it 100 times before, but do try to stick to a balanced diet which includes plenty of fresh fruit and vegetables.

● Try to drink at least six glasses of water a day. Water helps to cleanse your system of impurities and makes your hair and skin look extra healthy.

● Try to take some regular exercise such as swimming or aerobics – a boost to your circulation will help your hair shine.

● If you've been a bit off-colour or feel that you are lacking certain vitamins in your diet, try taking supplements. Kelp (powdered seaweed) can be taken in a handy tablet form and is well known for its beneficial effect on hair.

● Vitamin B complex is another hair shine goodie. This can be found in yeast extract, eggs, liver and wholegrains, or you can take it as a supplement in tablet form.

● While you're watching TV or as part of your shampoo routine, give your scalp a soothing massage. This helps to stimulate blood circulation and encourages healthy new hair growth.

● Cut down on sugary foods as they destroy vitamin B – as well as your teeth!

● All that fresh air may be good for you but make sure your hair's protected from the drying effects of sun and wind when you're out and about.

● Central heating will dry your hair and skin out – but if you can't live without it, treat yourself to a humidifier to put the moisture back into the air.

# FINISHING OFF

*Try these professional tricks for a photo finish.*

● Warm and soften a fingerful of hair wax using a hairdryer and smooth over your hair for the ultimate shine.

● Spritz a little finishing spray onto a comb and run it through your hair to prevent static.

● Add a drop of rosemary oil to your brush to stop tangles forming and eliminate static.

● Get instant gloss with a few drops of spray-on shine. Keep it light though, or you could end up looking like your hair needs a wash.

# IN A SLEEK CONDITION

*If your hair lacks shine make sure you:*

● Always use a conditioner.

● Treat your hair once a week to a deep conditioning treatment. Use a cream or wax formula and leave on for 30 minutes.

● Try a hot oil treatment if your hair is out of condition or your scalp dry. Warm a tablespoon of vegetable oil and massage into your hair. Wrap in cling film and leave on as long as possible before shampooing out.

● Make your own natural conditioner from mashed avocado, raw egg, natural yoghurt or home made mayonnaise. Leave on your hair for ½ hour and rinse well.

● Pour ½ a cup of cider vinegar over your hair as a finishing rinse after shampooing for sleek hair.

● If you're blonde, squeeze a lemon over your hair instead of conditioner – it'll pick up highlights as well as shine.

● Put your conditioner on while you're in the bath – the steam will make the treatment penetrate into your hair.

# DO THE SCRUN

**Scrunch-drying your hair is as easy as crumpling a piece of paper in your hand. Here's how to add a truly professional finish to short, medium and long styles**

Ever wished you could make your hair look as good at home as it does when you leave the salon? Well, there's one technique popular with hairdressers that's *really* easy to copy – it's called scrunch-drying and it's a great way of giving extra volume and bounce to your hair.

Scrunching works best on layered hair, but you can use the technique on one-length hair that isn't too long (chin to shoulder length is best), as well as short, or naturally curly hair. All you need is some styling mousse and a blow dryer. If your hair's short, or cut in a bob, your usual

## SCRUNCHING A BOB

*Use the scrunching technique on shoulder-length hair, and Bob's your uncle – you'll have a style that's full of body and bounce.*

**1** Start with freshly washed, towel-dried hair. Squirt an egg-sized blob of styling mousse into one hand. Choose firm hold mousse for fine/normal hair; normal hold for thick/coarse hair.

**2** Work about half the mousse into the roots on one side of your hair. Use the rest on the other side. Use both hands to make sure you spread it right down to the ends.

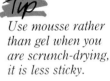
*Tip*
*Use mousse rather than gel when you are scrunch-drying, it is less sticky.*

**4** On a bob, scrunch from halfway down the length of the hair to the ends by literally screwing up a handful of hair in one hand. Hold for a count of five, aiming your hairdryer at the gaps between your fingers. Keep on scrunching all around your head.

**5** For maximum volume tip your head forwards and blow-dry the underneath of your hair using your fingers to lift and squeeze the roots. The finished effect should be tousled, soft and it should not look too neat.

*Tip*
*If the heat is too much for your fingers to bear, then it's too hot for your hair to handle!*

Photographs: LIZ McAULAY/Hair: LUKE at CAREY TEMPLE McADAM Make-up: KARIN DARNELL

# CH!

dryer will do, if it's long or curly, adding a diffuser attachment to the dryer will help.

All you have to do is work the mousse into your roots and scrunch your hair by screwing up handfuls of hair. Follow this up with a bit of clever blow-drying for a fantastic carefree style.

**3** Using your hairdryer on a medium heat, rough dry until your hair is only slightly damp. Use your fingers to lift the hair at the roots, pushing it back around your hairline to give lots of face-framing volume.

**6** When the finished effect looks exactly as you want it, set the style with a light mist of hairspray.

## Salon secrets

*For a scrunch that lasts, lift your hair and aim hairspray straight at the roots.*

## ANY QUESTIONS?

**Q** How do I know if my hair will suit scrunching?

**A** Scrunching suits just about any type of hair that has a wave. As long as your hair isn't too fine or completely shorn it should look great.

**Q** How long will the effects of scrunching last on my hair?

**A** Your hair should stay looking good all day. If you want it to last longer you can add a dot of wax. Rub this between the palms of both hands for even coverage.

**Q** Will scrunching do any damage?

**A** No. But if your hair is very dry, or over coloured, the heat from the hairdryer might. So if you're worried, dry your hair naturally, and then scrunch. Use a hairdryer on a low setting, and buy a special diffuser attachment to spread the heat.

# TWICE AS NICE

**1** Wash and towel-dry your hair. Comb a grapefruit-sized blob of mousse or a walnut-sized blob of gel evenly through your hair.

**2** Scrunch-dry the ends by grabbing handfuls of hair and gently lifting them up as you direct the air from the diffuser onto them. Don't dry the front yet.

**3** Comb the front of your hair into a quiff or wave. Hold it in place with a section clip. Make another two waves – behind the front one – and clip in place.

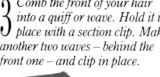
*Tip*

Add bags of body to your hair by tipping your head forwards and scrunch-drying the back.

**4** Point the hairdryer with diffuser attachment at the waves you have just made and dry them thoroughly. Leave your hair to cool.

**5** Remove the clips carefully without disturbing the waves. Fluff up the ends of your hair using your fingers. Tip your head forwards and shake it to add body.

*Personal styling guide*

◆ easy

🕐 quick to style

✳ **Works best on** one-length or layered wavy hair or any type of hair that scrunches easily.

☑ **You need:**
comb
mousse or gel
hairdryer with diffuser attachment
section clips

Photographs: NICK COLE/Hair: JUSTIN/Make-up: KAREN PURVIS/Top: NICK COLEMAN

# SCRUNCHING SHORT HAIR
*Short hair can benefit from a bit of bounce. Dry from the roots for extra lift.*

**BEFORE:**
*a short, straight cut.*

**1** ◄ **Work a small blob of mousse through damp hair. Grasp your hair firmly by the roots and lift as you dry. Use a hairdryer with a nozzle attachment.**

**2** ► **Keep drying the top layers until they are completely dry, and there you have it – a sophisticated style with body and lift.**

## HOT AIR DIFFUSER

This bowl-shaped hairdryer attachment is invaluable for drying curls without frizz. It's also gentler on your hair than a straightforward hairdryer. Some dryers are sold with a diffuser, but if you buy one separately, make sure it fits the dryer you've got at home!

# SCRUNCHING CURLS
*Scrunch-drying is not just for making waves, it's also a way of drying natural curls and perms.*

**1** *Use a blob of styling mousse on your hair. Firm hold is ideal for fine/normal hair, and normal hold for thick, permed hair.*

**2** *Work half the mousse well into the roots, then use your fingers to work the rest of the mousse through to the ends.*

**3** *Bend your head forwards and hold the hairdryer below your hair, so it's pointing upwards.*

**4** *Scrunch up handfuls of hair while you're drying it. To dry the top sections of hair, hold the dryer a couple of inches above your hair. Scrunch up handfuls until you have a headful of soft curls.*

Photographs: ADRIAN BRADBURY/Black top: PINEAPPLE

# MOUSSE, GEL, WAX & SPRAY

## Quick results from the best products for you

# SUPER MOUSSE

**Mousse makes light work of hair styling – for natural body and bounce, you'll find it's all in the can!**

These days if you want body, shape and manageability for your hair then you need look no further than a can of mousse. It's actually a setting agent in foam form. The foam helps spread it through your hair, then dissolves, leaving a fine coating of resins to help you shape your hair. Canned mousse also contains a chemical propellant which turns it from liquid to foam when it leaves the container. Help mix them into a firm foam with a quick shake before use. The latest mousses come in squeezy plastic bottles and are propellant-free. They use an air-pump which makes a light and fluffy mousse – and should not be shaken before use.

**GET IT RIGHT!**

For best results, always use the right amount of mousse – too little and the style will flop, too much and you'll make it dull and sticky.

- On short hair use an egg-sized blob of mousse.
- On medium-length, short Afro or permed hair, use an orange-sized blob.
- On long Afro, permed and very long straight hair, use a grape-fruit-sized blob.

Never put mousse straight on to your hair. Rub a small blob over your palms, then spread it through your hair. If you're using a big blob, scoop up a manageable amount and work into hair section by section.

## HEATWAVE

*Mousse doesn't just work when hair's wet – it can give dry hair a whole new look, too.*

## WHICH ONE TO CHOOSE

**Mousse comes in several different strengths – choose one to suit your hair and styling needs.
NORMAL HOLD – for daily use on normal hair.
EXTRA/SUPER HOLD – contains an extra bonding agent. Use it for elaborate styles or on very fine or flyaway hair.
CONDITIONING MOUSSE – leaves a sheen on your hair. Good choice if you blow-dry as the extra conditioners help protect your hair from the heat, but the conditioner may weaken the hold.**

1 *Massage an egg-sized blob of mousse thoroughly into your roots, pushing your hair back from your forehead as you go.*

2 *Comb through to spread the mousse from the roots to the ends and to encourage your hair to lie flat and smooth.*

Photographs: IAN HOOTON/Hair: PENNY ATTWOOD/Make-up: LIZZIE COURT/Vest: KNICKERBOX Silk Jacket: FRENCH CONNECTION/Earrings: NEC;CESSORY

**53**

**3** With clean palms, push the top section of your hair forwards into a gentle wave so that the hairline roots are lifted away from your forehead.

**4** Holding the wave in place, blow-dry on a high setting for two to three minutes to dry the mousse and set your hair.

# FRIZZ-FREE VOLUME

*Mousse keeps curls under control when blow-drying.*

**1** Towel-dry wet hair to remove excess water. Blot rather than rub it, which can roughen the surface and cause tangles.

## Watchpoint

Afro and permed hair is very porous so it will absorb mousse quickly. Don't judge by looks alone. Feel your hair – it should be slightly sticky, but not tacky.

## Tip

Don't worry if your hair's not squeaky clean, a little natural oil will give the style more staying power.

## Tip

Concentrated heat can harm your hair, so it's much safer to move the dryer away for a few moments to 'rest' in between hot blasts.

**4** Use a wide-toothed comb to spread the mousse evenly down the length of your hair.

**5** Blow-dry your hair using your fingers to shape and separate the curls. If the ends are still frizzy once it's dry rub in a marble-sized blob of mousse.

# SCRUNCH BUNCH

*If your hair's dry or damaged, it's kinder to wave it by hand!*

## Tip

If your hair is thick, it may still be damp after an hour's wrapping, so re-wrap it in a warmed dry towel to speed up the drying.

**1** Lightly towel-dry your hair to remove excess water. Blot away as much as you can to shorten the towel-wrap drying time later.

**2** Comb your hair back to get rid of any tangles. Squirt an orange-sized blob of mousse into one hand.

**3** Start to work the mousse through your hair by gently massaging it into the roots.

2 Squirt a grapefruit-sized blob of mousse into one hand. You'll need less if your hair is shorter than in our picture.

3 Dip your fingers in the mousse to give lots of small blobs. Massage these into the roots.

# MOUSSE MIX

*Polish up your act! Mix wax with mousse for super shine and extra sleek control.*

Rubbing wax thoroughly in your palms will warm and melt it slightly so it's much easier to use. If it's not warmed the wax may form thick clumps in your hair when you work it through.

1 Take a thumbnail-sized blob of wax and rub it between your palms until very smooth.

Body: KNICKERBOX / Top: HENNES / Cardigan: HENNES

# QUICK TIPS

● Mousses do vary – some are stickier than others, so you should use a little less; others are watery and you may need more than usual. To test a new mousse squirt a blob on to one hand, rub your palms together, then slowly pull them apart to see whether they feel tacky or watery.
● Work mousse into your hair quickly so it doesn't dry on your hands.
● Don't forget to spread the mousse on your back hair and along your hairline.

2 Rub an egg-sized blob of mousse into your waxed palms. Smooth it over your hair. 'Comb' moussed fingers through the ends to separate curls.

4 Work it through the ends of your hair by scrunching with moussed palms. This will encourage loose waves to form.

5 Take a warmed dry towel and wrap it around your head. Leave your hair to dry for about an hour.

6 Smooth a marble-sized blob of mousse over your fingers and give the dried curls a final scrunch into shape.

**BEFORE**
*Start with freshly-washed,
towel-dried hair.*

1 *Smooth an egg-sized blob of
mousse through your hair from
the roots to the ends.*

2 *Brush your hair through using
a vent brush to help spread the
mousse evenly.*

3 *Dry using your fingers to lift
hair up and away from your
head. Make sure you dry the
roots first to give maximum lift.*

4 *Tip your head forwards slightly
and dry the back section,
keeping the hairdryer pointing
upwards to give root lift.*

**Cropped hair can
reach the height
of fashion with
this spiky style.
Just arm yourself
with mousse and
a hairdryer
and go all out for
the high life**

# HAIR RAISER

5 *Continue to dry the front and
side sections in the same way,
remembering to lift the hair with
your fingers as you go.*

6 *Soften the fringe by putting the
flat side of the vent brush
against your forehead and gently
drying the hair over it.*

7 *Finish by working a marble-
sized blob of gel through the hair
to give shine and hold.*

**FINISHED**

Hair gel is good news for short styles, his and yours, to give lift, shape and long-lasting hold. Here's how to transform two basic cuts with just one tube of sticky stuff!

# GEL KNOW HOW

If you like to change your hairstyle as often as your clothes, then hair gel is for you! Just a handful of gel can sculpt, wave or set your hair into a style that will last from dawn until dusk. With a little imagination you can give a simple short cut a different look for every day of the week, according to your outfit or mood.

Gel is available in lots of different colours, none of which makes any difference to the end result. What does make a difference is the amount of gel that you put on – too little and your style won't stay, too much and you'll look as if you haven't washed your hair for a fortnight!

Work in gel sparingly and remember that you can always add more, but you can't take it away without washing your hair again.

## WHAT'S WHAT

All gel formulations can be used on towel-dried or dry hair.
**Normal hold**: for softer, overall hold. Use to emphasise a fringe or add texture to a layered cut.
**Extra hold**: for high hair and spiky styles. The best formulation for holding fine hair in place.
**Wet-look**: for slicked back, glossy styles. Remains pliable rather than setting rock hard.

57

# GEL FOR THE GIRLS

Dress: MISS SELFRIDGE/Earrings: HENNES

1 *Wash your hair and allow it to dry thoroughly before you start. Comb through.*

2 *Squeeze a marble-sized blob of gel into the palm of one hand. Rub your palms together to spread the gel.*

## KISS CURL GIRL

◄ Use enough gel to enable you to comb back your hair into a smooth, sleek finish. Section a triangle of hair on the front hairline, gel it and hold in a curl shape with your fingers until it dries. Avoid sticking the curl to your forehead and put on your make-up first so that you don't have to disturb your work of art!

## UPTOWN GIRL

► Look chic by sculpting and smoothing the front section of your hair up and over, using your fingers and palms to secure the shape while the gel dries. Finish by stroking and smoothing back the sides of your hair.

*If you're a regular gel user and your hair starts to look a little dull, switch to using an anti build-up shampoo until the shine returns.*

Blouse: NEXT/Jacket: MISS SELFRIDGE/Earrings: NEXT

*Tip*

*If gel leaves you looking as if you've got a bad attack of dandruff, you're probably using too much. Use only a thin film, rather than blobs which flake as they dry.*

## NEW WAVE

► For a more heavily sculptured look you will need to put on slightly more gel and comb it through. Slide your palm up and back across the side of your head and hold the wave in place with your hands until the gel has dried. Smooth back the sides, adding a touch more gel to tame any stray hairs.

## SOFT & GENTLE

▼ Use your fingers to flick your hair in all directions to achieve lift and volume. Now bring it all forwards from the back of your head into a full fringe. By adding a little more gel to some sections you can create different textures and movement.

*3 Put it on the roots of your hair first and then smooth it down to the ends with your fingers for an even coating.*

*4 A quick flick through with a comb and you're ready to start styling.*

### Tip

*If you've used a little gel to add texture and lift, this should disappear with a good brushing. If you've used a lot or a wet-look formulation you'll have to shampoo.*

**Cardigan: BENETTON**

**Top: HENNES/Earrings: NEXT**

# GEL TRICKS

## AFRO
Beat the frizzies by applying extra hold gel with your fingers, just to the ends, and pulling small strands of hair straight.

## PLAITS
Run a little gel along a finished plait to smooth down stray hairs and create a sleek look.

## VOLUME
Rub into the roots while your hair is still damp then finger-dry, directing the heat from the hair-dryer under rather than on top of your hair to give some lift.

## SLEEK
To cover up hair that's looking less than lovely, or to hide growing out layers, put gel on dry hair and comb into place. You'll need one marble-sized blob upto shoulder length and two blobs if it is any longer.

## BOBS
Smooth gel lightly over the surface of any one-length style, such as a bob, instead of hairspray.

## CURLS
Use a wet-look gel to smooth over permed or naturally curly hair to add a glossy shine and to separate the curls.

# GEL FOR THE BOYS

1 *Wash your hair and allow it to dry thoroughly before you start. Comb it through.*

2 *Squeeze a marbled-sized blob of gel into the palm of one hand and rub palms together.*

3 *Work the gel into your hair from the roots right to the ends with your fingertips.*

4 *Comb through lightly to get an even spread, and now it's time to get creative!*

### CITY SLICKER
◄ For a sleek finish apply another small blob of gel and comb through. Part your hair with a comb and shape the front section into an S-shaped wave. Comb the sides to lie smooth and flat about your ears.

### FLOWER POWER
◄ Lift your front hair up and over and hold in place with your hands until the gel dries. Using your palms, smooth back the sides and back of your hair. Tame strays hairs with a little extra gel.

### STYLE KING
► Lift the front section of hair up and over using your hands and hold in position until the gel dries. Pay special attention to smoothing the sides to create a contrast with the lifted top piece. To achieve the cross-over look, smooth the sides to meet at the back.

Photographs: ADRIAN BRADBURY/Hair: MIA/Make-up: TRACEY LERMAN/Man's waistcoat and shirt: NEXT/Red jacket: MONSOON/Dresses: MISS SELFRIDGE/Earrings: HARVEY NICHOLS

# WAX FACTOR

**Wax'll fix it when it comes to shaping and smoothing your hair – for both guys and girls. Get it right and you'll be sleeks ahead with the ultimate in shine**

Wax is the up-to-date version of what used to be known as hair dressing by your grandad. It's a mix of waxes and oils that adds softness, body and shine to your hair without leaving it greasy.

Hair wax is water resistant so you can't use it on wet hair. It can also be fairly difficult to wash out unless it's a water-soluble wax so check the label before you buy. However, it works wonders on all types of freshly dried hair as it's strong enough to structure curls, add root lift and smooth for a perfect, professional finish.

If you use mousse, gel or setting lotion put wax on styled and dried hair to stop it looking dull. And you can restore the shine to hair that has lost its lustre thanks to perming or colouring with – you guessed! – wax.

*If you want to get rid of a non-water soluble wax put a little shampoo on dry hair, massage well then wash as usual.*

# GET IT ON

*The way you put wax on your hair makes all the difference when you're after a stylish, non-greasy effect.*

Jacket and dress: MONSOON/Earrings: COROCRAFT

**Tip**

Keep the lid tightly closed if you don't want a pot of wax to harden.

1 If the wax is too solid, gently warm it with a hairdryer on a cool setting until the surface is slightly runny.

2 Start with just a thumbnail-sized blob. You can always add more if you need to.

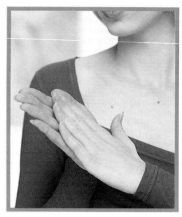

3 Always spread the wax over your hands first. This warms the wax and makes it easier to smooth evenly over your hair.

**Watchpoint**

Only use wax on really clean hair as it will make hair greasy if there's any excess natural oils.

## FINGER CURLS

◄ Wax coated hair can quickly and easily be moulded into face framing curls. Just smooth some wax through the hair then take 12 mm/½ in sections and twist into individual curls with your fingers. Set with a hair-dryer on a cool setting, then pull the curls forwards and arrange them to frame your face.

**Watchpoint**

If you're prone to oily skin don't bring waxed hair forwards on to your face.

62

*Watchpoint*

*Don't sleep on it! When you use wax make sure that you shampoo your hair before you hit the pillow or you'll suffer the greasy consequences in the morning!*

## BOUNCE FOR BOYS

◄ Add shape to a short layered cut with a touch of wax. Allow the hair to dry naturally, then coax it into shape with a small amount of wax paying particular attention to the front and sides. Smooth your hands through from roots to ends so that the finished effect doesn't look too solid.

## MAKING WAVES

► Use a little more wax and add some rippling waves. Start at the front hairline and run wax back through your hair. Push the top section forwards into a wave with one hand, and secure with three long clips. Fix the waves in place with a hairdryer on a gentle heat setting.

*Tip*

*Banish a wispy hairline with just a little wax when you've finished creating a neat upswept style.*

## CURL UP

◄ Wax adds definition and texture to naturally curly and permed hair. Lightly massage the wax through short hair with lots of curls, starting at the roots. Use your fingers to lift the front section to flatter your face, then gently tease the curls into shape. The result is curls with added body and texture as well as long lasting hold.

## FRIZZ FREE

▶ Wax is Afro hair's best friend, helping to separate the curls, add shine and beat the frizzies. Spread wax evenly through your hair, from roots to ends. Working in small sections literally 'squeeze' the wax into your hair until you've eliminated frizziness and defined the curls.

*Wax smoothes down the surface of the hair and helps prevent static electricity that makes it frizz.*

## SMOOTH OPERATOR

◀ Use wax to smooth down stray hairs on a sleek style and add a healthy shine. Blow-dry your hair in the usual way, then run wax-coated hands over the surface. Use the remaining wax on your hands to lightly separate the fringe, and you'll have a glossy look that's ultra-sophisticated. It's also a great way to give damaged hair gloss too.

# HOLDING POWER

**Hairspray used to be stiff stuff, but it now gives a much more natural look. And it's versatile – use it to set your style, hold it, add body or control flyaway ends**

Hairsprays are still the best-selling hair styling product – and most fall into one of two main categories – traditional 'holding' sprays which fix hair, or the newer styling sprays. Some, however, cleverly combine both actions.

Holding hairsprays come in either aerosols or pump action sprays. Most aerosols are now free of CFCs – the chemicals that threaten the ozone layer. Almost all styling sprays come in pump action packs.

Aerosols discharge a very fine mist, which dries quickly. Pump action hairsprays tend to come out quite wet, so need a couple of seconds in which to dry. These can be too heavy for fine hair.

Holding sprays are available in various strengths: normal/natural, extra firm, or mega-hold. The stronger the hold, the more alcohol and resins in the spray.

The closer you hold the nozzle to your head, the wetter the spray will be and the firmer the hold it will give. Hold aerosols at least 15 cm/6 in away.

## ON THE SHELF

Confused by all the choices in the shops? Our guide will help you:

**AEROSOL HAIRSPRAY** Use to give support to your style, and as finishing spray. It's suitable for all hair types, especially fine or floppy hair.

**CONDITIONING HAIRSPRAY** Acts like hairspray, but contains conditioners, which make it good for chemically-treated and dry hair. It also adds shine.

**STYLING SPRAY** Usually comes in a pump action pack and can be used on damp hair to shape and on dry hair to hold. Many also contain conditioners. It's good for all hair types. Also known as styling spritz, sculpting mist, fixing spray or spray fix.

**VOLUMISING SPRAY** Unlike most sprays, which just coat the outside of the hair shaft, this type penetrates the follicle to give inner strength. Special resins coat each strand to thicken hair. It also styles either dry or damp hair. It's good for all hair types, especially fine, flyaway hair needing body.

**SPRAY-ON SHINE** This is similar to a conditioning hairspray and will add lustre to your finished look. Some brands combine spray-on shine with holding power.

# SLEEK IS CHIC

For a chic chignon, plait or French pleat, use spray-on shine to give hair a sleek finish and help fight static.

**1** Comb holding spray through clean, dry hair before you start.

For a smooth finish, make the hair quite wet with spray before you style it.

**2** When you've put your hair up as you want it, use a spray-on shine to give it gloss. This will also help to hold hair.

### Watchpoint

Touch-up with spray from a distance – if the hair gets too wet strands will separate.

**3** A good squirt of spray round the hairline will stop stray hairs from escaping and spoiling the sleek line.

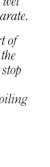

As you spray, smooth hair with your free hand to keep straggly strands in place.

# FAST FORWARD

To achieve a textured look on short hair, use a volumising spray.

**1** Start with hair that's clean and dry. Tip your head forwards and work volumising spray through to the roots.

**2** Lift and mould the hair into shape with your fingers then lightly spritz with holding spray to fix in place.

# SMART GIRLS KEEP IT SMOOTH

For a really sleek head of hair, use sprays to build in body and give a smooth finish.

### Tip

Even sleek styles need movement, so hair mustn't be set like concrete. The secret is not to be too heavy-handed with spray – lightly does it!

**1** Make sure your hair is freshly-washed, towel-dried and free of tangles before you start to style it.

**3** Blow-dry hair back off your face, using a round brush. Follow the brush with your hairdryer for a smooth finish.

**4** Now spritz with an aerosol hairspray, brushing it through from the roots to keep all hair smooth.

3 The finished result is a textured look that you can just fluff up again to revive.

## LOOSEN UP

For a tousled look combine rough-drying with a volume spray.

1 Start with towel-dried hair. Spritz with volumising spray, then tip your head to the side. Rough-dry with a hairdryer.

2 Dry all your hair in the same way, using your fingers to style and shape.

2 Run a vent brush through your hair, from roots to ends, at the same time spritzing with volumising spray.

## FINISHING TOUCHES

After setting your hair on heated rollers, lightly spritz with hairspray all over to help set the curls.

To give any style a less 'set' looking finish, squirt hairspray onto a brush, then run quickly through your hair before it dries.

*Tip*

Give a bob a sleek finish by spritzing hair lightly with hairspray then smoothing the hair under with your hand.

5 Set the finished style with a fine mist of hairspray all over. Smooth down any stray hairs with the palm of your hand.

# STRAIGHT TO THE POINT

*Smooth your fringe into pointed tips for a cheeky, impish look.*

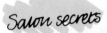

*Salon secrets*

For a really smooth finish, reverse your comb and use the back instead of the teeth.

1 *Make a parting, if you wear one, then comb your hair smooth, following closely with a fine mist of styling spray.*

# BACK TO YOUR ROOTS

*Give lift to longer styles.*

1 *Squirt holding spray directly at the hair between your fingers.*

2 *Tease out the curls at the ends of your hair, then use more spray to fix the style. Spray upwards so the style doesn't flop.*

2 *Spritz the fringe with spray, teasing strands of hair into points with your fingers.*

3 *The finished look draws attention to the eyes and flatters a fuller face.*

*Watchpoint*

If you have an elaborate style which needs a lot of spray to hold it, you may need to wash your hair more often to get rid of the build-up.

# SCRUNCH IT UP

*For a crisp, even curl on a layered bob, forget mousse and reach for the styling spray.*

*Tip*

Using spray rather than mousse to scrunch-dry fine, flyaway hair leaves it lots lighter.

1 *Wash and towel-dry your hair, then tip your head forwards and squirt all over with styling spray, working it into the roots.*

2 *Rough-dry all over with a hairdryer, then scrunch-dry by screwing up handfuls of hair and directing the dryer on to it.*

3 *The finished look shouldn't be too tight or too tousled. When it's just right, spritz with hairspray to hold.*

# UPTOWN CURL

**If your hair feels limp and lank then heat up your rollers and give yourself a headful of waves fit for a film star. You'll soon be ready to take on a starring rôle!**

**BEFORE**
*Wash and dry your hair.*

1 *Warm up your rollers then take a 5 cm/2 in wide section from the back of the crown, comb through and spray with hairspray.*

2 *Hold a roller about 5 cm/2 in above your head and wrap your hair around it to encourage more curl at the roots.*

3 *Tuck any stray ends under the roller with the tail of a styling comb, and then secure with a roller pin.*

*Tip*

*If you can't get the ends of your hair to stay put, wrap end papers around them before you fix the rollers to your head.*

4 *Continue to wind rollers in horizontal sections down the back of your hair.*

5 *When you've finished winding up the rollers, leave them in for 10 minutes before removing. Then leave the curls to cool.*

6 *Run your fingers gently through your hair to loosen the curls into waves.*

7 *Finish with a light spritz of spray-on shine. Be careful not to use too much or the curls will sag and hang flat.*

**FINISHED**

**SIMPLE STYLES**

Easy, step-by-step hairstyles
for you to try

# PERM HOLD!

**BEFORE**
*Start with dry hair, spritz with hairspray to give it extra hold.*

**Here's a topping idea for perking up your perm and livening up those layers**

*Personal styling guide*

◆ *easy*

🕐 *quick to style*

✳ **Works best on** *permed or naturally curly hair that's chin-length or longer. Hair should be layered.*

☑ **You need:**
*hairspray*
*hairpins*
*round brush*

**FINISHED**

1 *Loosely take one side of your hair round to the back of your head and pin down the centre. Spritz with hairspray.*

2 *Using a round brush, gently back-brush the front hair to add volume and height to the style.*

3 *Roll the length of your hair back to the centre and pin in place. Leave any stray ends loose.*

4 *Wind any loose tendrils around your finger and spritz with hairspray to hold the curl. The front should look tousled.*

Photographs: ALISTAIR HUGHES/Hair: JANE FOSTER/Make-up: VANESSA HAINES/Top: PINEAPPLE

# FRENCH PLEAT

**Pack a Parisian punch by updating a classic French pleat for a simple style that's the ultimate in continental chic**

**BEFORE**
*Start with clean dry hair.*

1 — *Section off your hair at the front and clip out of the way – you'll work on this hair last.*

2 — *Smooth on a touch of hair wax for sleekness and comb the rest of your hair into a ponytail at the back of your head.*

*Tip*

*If your hair's fine, help the pleat to last by securing it with a line of criss-cross grips.*

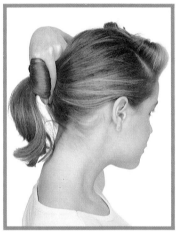

3 — *Loop the ponytail firmly around your index finger and smooth with your comb.*

5 — *Still holding firmly, twist your hand around until the hair on the outside of the roll is lying smooth. Secure with pins.*

6 — *Clean up any stray hairs by smoothing over with your tailcomb and hand.*

7 — *Unpin the front section and back-comb lightly to add lift. Smooth back, keeping some wave in the hair.*

8 — *Tuck the ends of your fringe into the top of the pleat with your tailcomb. Put a grip in and spritz with hairspray.*

Photographs: ADRIAN BRADBURY/Hair: LAURA for JOHN FRIEDA/Make-up: VIRGINIA NICHOLS/Top: MARY QUANT/Earrings: RIO

4 *Loop your hair around again until the ends are tucked in.*

**FINISHED**

*Personal styling guide*

◆◆ *some skill required*

🕐🕐 *can't be hurried*

✳ **Works best on** *straight or wavy shoulder-length hair.*

☑ **You need:**
*tailcomb*

*hair grips*
*hair clips*
*styling wax*
*hairspray*

*Watchpoint*

*The pleat will look too bulky if your hair's long and thick.*

## Personal styling guide

◆ ◆ *some skill required*

🕐 🕐 *can't be hurried*

✳ **Works best on** *medium thick hair that is long on top and short at the back and the sides.*

☑ **You need:**
*heat styling lotion*
*tongs*
*vent brush*
*hairspray*
*wax*

### Tip

*Always use a heat styling lotion when you use tongs.*

# TONG-IN-CHIC

**Give your hair a lift! Transform a smooth, long-layered style into masses of bubbly curls. It doesn't take long to master the technique – the secret lies in tonging the curls randomly**

**BEFORE**
*Make sure your hair is clean and completely dry before you begin to style it.*

Photographs: PAUL MITCHELL/Hair: SHAUN GLOAG/
Make-up: LIZZIE COURT/Swimsuit: HENNES/Jacket: TOP SHOP

1 *Take a small section of hair from the back of your crown and spray lightly with heat styling lotion.*

2 *Wrap the sprayed section around the heated styling tongs and hold in place for 30 seconds.*

3 *Continue to make curls all over your head at random, positioning the curls so that there are no obvious partings.*

4 *Carefully brush the curls away from your face using a vent brush.*

**FINISHED**

5 *Once you've arranged your hair just as you want it, fix the top in place with your usual hairspray.*

6 *Using your vent brush again, brush the sides of your hair backwards, sweeping it behind your ears.*

7 *Put a little hair wax on your fingertips and use it to break up your curls which will then take on a natural, shining look.*

**BEFORE**
*Don't shampoo for 24 hours before styling – natural oil will help.*

1 *Work a grapefruit-sized blob of mousse through the entire length of your hair. Dry the roots with your hairdryer.*

2 *Scrunch-dry the ends – lift the hair up in your fingers and scrunch it loosely to encourage the waves.*

# TURN UP THE VOLUME

**Long waves are where it's at! So get turned on to scrunch-drying and back-combing and make your stye a resounding success**

**FINISHED**
**Hair has bags of body and great-looking waves.**

3 *Scrunch-dry top hair, then begin back-combing. Comb the hair around your face at the roots to create maximum body.*

4 *Continue back-combing all the hair. Then spritz with plenty of hairspray at the roots to hold the back-combing in place.*

**BEFORE**
*Make sure your hair is clean
and dry before you start. Find
your natural parting.*

*Personal styling
guide*

◆◆     *some skill required*

🕐🕐     *can't be hurried*

✳ **Works best on**
*shoulder length or longer
hair.*

☑ **You will need:**
*heat styling lotion
hairdryer
curling tongs
hair grips
Afro comb*

 *Tip*

*If some of your back hair is
too short to gather up, spritz
with hairspray and smooth it
upwards to keep it in place.*

1 Spray heat styling lotion through your hair. Set tongs to heat up. Rough-dry with a hairdryer for two minutes.

**If your hair is neither long nor short but at that awkward in-between stage, don't let it get you down. Give yourself an instant lift with a topknot of tumbling curls**

# CURLS ON TOP

2 Starting at the crown, take an 8 cm/3 in wide section and wind it onto the tongs. Hold for 30 seconds for a firm curl.

3 Keeping the sausage-roll shape of the curl, secure it with a hair grip before starting to tong the rest of your hair.

4 Tong all over your hair so the curls lie in a random pattern, securing each curl as you go.

5 Unclip the curls and gently work them loose with your fingers. Try not to pull them out of shape.

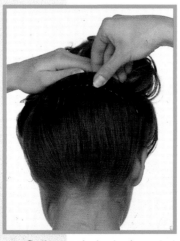

6 Twist the side sections over once and gather up on top of your head. Secure with grips, leaving the curled ends free.

7 Gather up the back of your hair in the same way, and use a wide, curved comb to give a smooth, secure finish.

8 Finally, gently tease the front curls with a wide-toothed comb to soften the fringe.

80

**BEFORE**
*Comb through clean, dry hair to remove any knots and tangles. Spray lightly with styling spray.*

Feeling flat? Don't hide away behind a lank fringe. Smarten up your act – and give yourself a lift – by tonging your hair into an upwardly mobile curly top

# STICK UP!

*Tip*

1 *Part your hair into 2.5 cm/1 in wide sections. Lift each vertically from your head and tong into sausage-shaped curls.*

2 *Continue curling section by section until all the hair has been tonged into curls.*

*For lasting hold on naturally straight or very fine hair finish off with a squirt of extra hold styling spray.*

**FINISHED**

3 *Separate the curls by running your fingers vigorously through the hair, then tip your head forwards and blow-dry the roots.*

4 *A thumbnail-sized blob of styling wax worked through the hair will shape and separate the curls to finish the style.*

# TWIST IN THE TAIL

**Make some-fin more of your long hair with this elegant fishbone plait. Simply follow our guide and we're sure you'll soon be hooked on this look. So go on and splash out in style!**

Photographs: ADRIAN BRADBURY/Hair: PENNY ATTWOOD/Make-up: SHARON IVES/Top: MISS SELFRIDGE/Earrings: CRYSTALIZE

**BEFORE**
*Make sure your hair is well brushed before you start.*

1 *Spritz your hair lightly with hairspray and brush it through thoroughly. This will help prevent static and give your plait a much neater finish.*

2 *Brush your hair over to one side then gather it into a ponytail, securing it with a covered elastic band. Take a strand of hair and wind it around the band, tuck in the end and secure with a hair grip.*

3 *Separate the ponytail into two bunches, then take a thin strand of hair from the outer section of each bunch.*

4 *Take the thin strand from the left-hand bunch over to the right and incorporate into the right-hand bunch.*

5 *Next take the thin strand from the right-hand bunch over to the left and incorporate into the left-hand bunch.*

some skill required

 can't be hurried

**✳ Works best on** *hair that's all one length.*

☑ **You need:**
*hairbrush
hairspray
covered elastic bands
hair grips*

*If your hair's curly or wavy blow-dry it first for a smooth finish.*

6 *Continue plaiting in this way down the length of hair taking in new strands as you work. Fasten the ends securely with a covered elastic band.*

# CURLS AHEAD

**BEFORE**
*It's a sleek bob and in good condition, but sometimes it's nice to have a complete change.*

**Got a dead straight bob and thought you could do nothing with it? It might be sleek and smooth, but now's the time for a change. So get ahead, get a grip and get some curl!**

Photographs: ALISTAIR HUGHES/Hair: JANE FOSTER/Make-up: VANESSA HAINES/Blouse: LAURA ASHLEY

1 *Switch on your tongs to heat up. Rub a marble-sized blob of gel through the length of your hair, being careful to distribute it evenly.*

2 *Tong 2.5 cm/1 in-thick sections of hair into ringlets. Grip each ringlet to your head to help set the curl.*

3 *When you have tonged and gripped all the hair, leave it to cool down completely and then take out the grips.*

4 *Run your fingers through your hair to break the curl and, if it's still damp, scrunch-dry it with your hands and a hairdryer.*

5 *Starting at one side, roll hair back behind your ear and loosely grip. Repeat on other side. Continue rolling up the rest of the hair.*

6 *Ruffle the front of the hair loosely into shape and spritz lightly with hairspray to hold the style in place.*

# PILE UP!

**Go for the high life and tease wavy hair into luscious, tumbling curls.**

**Quick and easy to style, it's worth a try if you're a girl who wants to be top of the pile!**

**BEFORE**
*This style looks great on wavy, one-length hair.*

1 *Work through an egg-sized blob of mousse from roots to ends.*

2 *Scrunch-dry your hair, attaching a diffuser to your hairdryer. For extra lift, tilt your head to the side.*

3 *Starting at one side, rake your hand through your hair taking it up towards the top of your head. Secure with a comb, letting any loose ends tumble over.*

4 *Repeat at the back and other side of the head. Then gently ruffle and tease your hair into shape.*

Photographs: NICK COLE/Make-up: KAREN PURVIS/Hair: JUSTIN/Jacket: NICK COLEMAN

**BEFORE**
*Hair should be clean and dry. Put your tongs on to heat.*

1 Comb hair through, then take 5 cm/2 in sections and start winding around the tongs from the ends to the roots.

*Tip*

Clamp the tongs at the very end of each section of hair to prevent kinks.

*Personal styling guide*

◆◆ some skill required

🕐🕐 can't be hurried

✳ **Works best on** jaw to shoulder-length

hair that's naturally wavy or curls easily.

☑ **You need:**
comb
tongs
hairspray
hair wax
hairpins

*Tip*

If your hair is very curly scrunch-dry it rather than curling with tongs.

# UP AND OVER

**A classic bob looks lovely left loose, but if you want to be more daring try tonging in curls — then rolling them off your face for a really fabulous finish!**

2 As you wind, place a comb through each section so that it lies flat against the scalp to protect it from the heat. Hold for 30 seconds.

3 When you have tonged all your hair, gently ruffle your hair with your fingers to break up the curl and give added volume.

4 Gather up one side of your hair and roll back and tuck. Use hairpins to secure the roll in place. Repeat on the other side.

5 When you have rolled both sides finish the back of the hair by running your fingers through to fan the hair out.

6 Finally, style the front section. For added shine, rub a little wax on your fingertips and run them through your hair.

**FINISHED**

Photographs: NICK COLE/Hair: PENNY ATTWOOD/Make-up: LIZZIE COURT/Top: PINEAPPLE/Earrings: HENNES

**BEFORE**
*Hair is slightly wavy at the ends.*

*1 Put the tongs on to heat up. Massage an orange-sized blob of mousse through slightly damp hair – working from the roots to the ends.*

*2 Rough-dry your hair with a hairdryer. Make sure it's completely dry all over before you start tonging.*

*3 Taking 2.5 cm/1 in sections, tong the underneath nape hair first, then work up towards the crown. Hold each curl for around 10 seconds.*

*4 Continue to tong all your hair – working round to the front until you have masses of sausage-shaped curls.*

*5 Break the curls up into gentle waves by running your fingers through them. Don't brush your hair – you'll pull the curl out.*

*6 The finished look – the full curls hide a frizzy, growing-out perm. Spritz with hairspray to hold the curls in place.*

# SHARP TONGED!

**With a flick of the tongs you can transform a wilting perm into perfect curls**

## Personal styling guide

◆ *easy*

⏰⏰ *can't be hurried*

✳ **Works best on**
*Chin-to shoulder-length hair that's slightly wavy or with a growing-out perm.*

☑ **You need:**
*heated tongs
mousse
hairdryer
hairspray*

91

**BEFORE**
*Clean roots are essential because they're going to be on display. Brush your hair thoroughly first.*

*1 Dampen hair all over with a water spray, then work an orange-sized blob of mousse through from the roots to the ends.*

*2 Rough dry hair using a hot setting on your dryer to create texture and body.*

*3 Use your fingers to sweep your hair up into a ponytail on your crown. Fasten with a covered elastic band.*

*4 Divide the ponytail into two equal sections and gently tug to make sure the root hair is pulled tight.*

*5 Wind one section over and around the base of the other section. Tuck ends under at the back and hold with hairpins.*

*6 Lift the second section so that it crosses over the back of the first one. Loop hair round then tuck ends under neatly. Use hairpins to hold hair in place.*

*7 Back-comb the roots of your fringe, then comb it over to one side so that it forms a quiff.*

# DOUBLE CROSSER!

**Feel you need to smarten up your act a little? Step into the spotlight with this glamorous, upswept style and give long hair a dual role**

◆ *easy*

⏱ *quick to style*

✳ **Works best on**
*below shoulder-length hair with a long fringe.*

☑ **You need:**
*mousse*

covered elastic band
hairpins
comb
hairspray

*This style must look neat at the back. Ask a friend to help if you find it tricky.*

**8** *Spritz hair with hairspray. Press your fingers gently against your hair as the spray dries to set the style in place.*

**FINISHED**
*You'll have twice the fun with this super slick style!*

*Tip*

*Buy yourself a pair of big loop earrings – they're the best thing to balance the style!*

Photographs: MATTHEW SMITH/Hair: PENNY ATTWOOD/Make-up: KAREN PURVIS/Top: FRENCH CONNECTION

# TOP LOOK

**Two in one – a body-building style that's worth its weight in gold. Plus a slicker version that's only a brush-stroke away. With either one you're hall-marked for success!**

Photographs: ALISTAIR HUGHES/Make-up: NICOLA ROSS/Hair: PAULA MANN/Tops: MARY QUANT, WAREHOUSE Blouse: WAREHOUSE/Earrings: ACCESSORIZE, TRIFARI

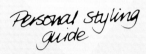

*Personal styling guide*

◆ *easy*

🕑 *quick to style*

✳ **Works best on** *medium to thick, one-length hair.*

☑ **You need:**
*mousse*
*diffuser*
*hairdryer*
*comb*
*hairspray*
*brush*

**BEFORE**
*Hair should be clean but does not need to be newly-washed.*

1 *Squeeze out an orange-sized blob of mousse and work it right through your hair so all the strands are evenly covered.*

2 *Use a diffuser attachment on your hairdryer and scrunch-dry. Direct the air jet from below to create width.*

3 *Lifting your hair away from your scalp, back-comb it all over using a fine-toothed comb. This will help create volume.*

4 *Spritz the roots of your hair with your favourite hairspray. Drop your head forward to get fullness at the back.*

5 *Use your fingers to position your hair away from your face for a fabulous backswept look. Spritz with hairspray again.*

**FINISHED**
One last spritz of hairspray gives this simple style a top salon look.

**ALTERNATIVE**
For a smoother look that keeps the volume, use a smidgen of gel and brush your hair behind your ears.